HENRY VAUGHAN AND THE
HERMETIC PHILOSOPHY

HENRY VAUGHAN
AND THE HERMETIC PHILOSOPHY

By ELIZABETH HOLMES, M.A., B.Litt.

Author of *Some Aspects of Elizabethan Imagery*

NEW YORK / RUSSELL & RUSSELL

FIRST PUBLISHED IN 1932
REISSUED, 1967, BY RUSSELL & RUSSELL
A DIVISION OF ATHENEUM HOUSE INC.
BY ARRANGEMENT WITH BASIL BLACKWELL, OXFORD
L. C. CATALOG CARD NO: 66−24708

PRINTED IN THE UNITED STATES OF AMERICA

EDITIONS USED IN THIS ESSAY

AGRIPPA, H. CORNELIUS.

> *Three Books of Occult Philosophy.* Trans. J.F. London, 1651.

BOEHME, JACOB.

> *XL Questions Concerning the Soule.* Trans. J. Sparrow. London, 1647.
> *The Three Principles of the Divine Essence.* Trans. J. Sparrow. London, 1648.
> *The Threefold Life of Man.* Trans. J. Sparrow. London, 1650.
> *Signatura Rerum.* Trans. J. Ellistone. London, 1651.
> *Concerning the Election of Grace.* Trans. J. Sparrow. London, 1655.
> *Aurora.* Trans. J. Sparrow. London, 1656.

BROWNE, SIR THOMAS.

> *Religio Medici.* London, 1643.
> *Hydriotaphia.* London, 1658.

BUNYAN, JOHN.

> *The Pilgrim's Progress. Grace Abounding,* etc. Ed. E. Venables. Second Edition. Oxford, 1900.

CRASHAW, RICHARD.

> *The Poems of Richard Crashaw.* Ed. L. C. Martin. Oxford, 1927.

CROLLIUS, OSWALD.

> *The Mysteries of Nature.* Trans. H. Pinnell. In *Philosophy Reformed and Improved in Four Tractates.* London, 1657.

v

DONNE, JOHN.

The Poems of John Donne. Ed. H. J. C. Grierson. Oxford, 1912.
Essayes in Divinity. London, 1651.
LXXX Sermons. London, 1640.
Fifty Sermons. London, 1648.
XXVI Sermons. London, 1664.

DREXELIUS, HIEREMIAS.

The Angel-Guardian's Clock. Trans. T.E.H. Rouen, 1650.

FOX, GEORGE.

A Journal. London, 1694.

GLANVILLE, JOSEPH.

Lux Orientalis. London, 1662.

HERBERT, GEORGE.

The English Works of George Herbert. Ed. G. H. Palmer. 3 vols. London, 1905.

HERMETICA.

Hermetica. Ed. W. Scott. 3 vols. Oxford, 1924.

HERMETIC MUSEUM, THE.

The Hermetic Museum. Trans. from the Latin original of Frankfurt, 1678. Preface, A. E. Waite. London, 1893.

MARVELL, ANDREW.

The Poems and Letters of Andrew Marvell. Ed. H. M. Margoliouth. 2 vols. Oxford, 1927.

MONTAIGNE, MICHAEL DE.

The Essays of Montaigne. Trans. J. Florio. 1603. Tudor Translations. Ed. W. E. Henley. 3 vols. London, 1893.

MORE, HENRY.

Platonica. Including, with separate pagination, *Psychozoia ; Psychathanasia ; Antipsychopannychia ; Antimonopsychia.* Cambridge, 1642.
An Antidote against Atheism. Fourth Edition. London, 1712.

NIEREMBERG, JOHN EUSEBIUS.
> *Of Adoration in Spirit and in Truth.* Trans. R.S. (S.J.). 1673.

PARACELSUS, THEOPHRASTUS.
> *The Hermetic and Alchemical Writings of Paracelsus the Great.* Ed. A. E. Waite. 2 vols. London, 1894.

SEBONDE, RAYMOND DE.
> *Theologia Naturalis siue liber creaturarum.* Daventrie : Rychardus paffroed. [c. 1480.]

TRAHERNE, THOMAS.
> *Centuries of Meditations.* Ed. B. Dobell. London, 1908.
> *Traherne's Poems of Felicity.* Ed. H. I. Bell. Oxford, 1910.

VAUGHAN, HENRY.
> *The Works of Henry Vaughan.* Ed. L. C. Martin. 2 vols. Oxford, 1914.

VAUGHAN, THOMAS.
> *Anima Magica Abscondita.* By Eugenius Philalethes. London, 1650.
> *Anthroposophia Theomagia.* By Eugenius Philalethes. London, 1650.
> *Magia Adamica . . . Whereunto is added Coelum Terrae.* By Eugenius Philalethes. London, 1650.
> *Lumen de Lumine.* By Eugenius Philalethes. London, 1651.

WEIGEL, VALENTINE.
> *Astrologie Theologized.* London, 1649.

DATES IN THE LIFE OF HENRY VAUGHAN

Born 17 April, 1622, at Newton-by-Usk, Brecknock-shire.

Taught (with his twin-brother Thomas) by Matthew Herbert, rector of Llangattock.

Went to Jesus College, Oxford, 1638, and studied law ; but left Oxford without taking a degree (Thomas Vaughan also went to Jesus College, and graduated there).

Began to practise as physician in Brecknock.c. 1645.

(1640 Thomas Vaughan presented to living of St. Bridget's, Brecknockshire. 1647 (?) deprived of his living, and removed to Oxford. Died 1666.)

Was at Newton again c. 1650, and continued there as physician.

Died 23 April, 1695.

A TABLE OF THE WORKS OF HENRY VAUGHAN

Poems, with the tenth Satyre of Juvenal, 1646.

Silex Scintillans, 1650.

Olor Iscanus (ready 1647, not published till) 1651, including, under one title-page (translations),
Of the Benefit Wee may get by our Enemies,
Of the Diseases of the Mind and the Body,
The Praise and Happinesse of the Countrie-Life.

The Mount of Olives : or, *Solitary Devotions,* 1652, including (translations),
Man in Darkness, or, *A Discourse of Death,*
Man in Glory.

Flores Solitudinis, 1654, comprising (translations),
Of Temperance and Patience,
Of Life and Death,
The World Contemned,
Primitive Holiness, set forth in the Life of Blessed Paulinus.

Silex Scintillans, 1655 (including the Second Part).

Hermetical Physick, 1655.

Thalia Rediviva, 1678 (including some verse-translations of the metres of Boethius).

Olor Iscanus, 1679.

HENRY VAUGHAN AND THE
HERMETIC PHILOSOPHY

I

THE reader of this short essay is invited to share in summary the results of an acquaintance with Henry Vaughan pursued a few steps further than the anthologies or even the histories of literature have gone. Vaughan's last and completest editor, Professor L. C. Martin, to whom I owe very much in the way of help and interest, has, in the notes to his edition, shown the path to such a deepened acquaintance ; and has himself progressed in most directions further than I can go. I have added to his researches in one direction mainly—that of Henry Vaughan's connection with the Hermetic or ' occult ' philosophy which his brother Thomas embraced and practised, and so of the poet's relations with his brother and possibly with others of the Hermetic manner of belief, notably Jacob Boehme, but also Cornelius Agrippa, Paracelsus, and others of obscurer name. The explanation suggested here as to the nature of Vaughan's religious experience is put forward on my own responsibility.

Mr. Edmund Blunden's little book on Vaughan[1] appeared about the time that I began to read in the Hermetic writers. A reading, and still more a recent re-reading, of that book convinced me that in Blunden, himself a metaphysical poet, Vaughan has found a critic whose ability to appreciate proceeds from a real

[1] *On the Poems of Henry Vaughan* (London, 1927).

friendship of spirit. I note too in his book some of my own findings about Vaughan, though he stresses more than I the gaiety of the poet, his humour, and the rapture of his ' starry, fountained, infinite dream.'[1] I have tried to discover some sources of that dream ; and found Vaughan, like some other metaphysical poets, a creature of conflict, though conflict of perhaps a different nature from theirs, and tending to become resolved in the alchemy of his mystical poetry.

The explanation which these pages seek to initiate, not complete, shows Vaughan's mysticism, however, to be of a special kind, and of a mixed culture. Various traditions meet in this writer. They are confused, the reader of his poetry cannot perhaps at first disentangle them ; yet if some clues are given he is surprised to find not only what variety of threads are apparent, but also how much clearer on this analysis the pattern looks. He need no longer describe Henry Vaughan vaguely as a ' Nature-mystic,' or a forerunner of Wordsworth only, or on other preferences as a devout Anglican, close follower of George Herbert ; or as an aspirant to the contemporary metaphysical school in verse ; but he may find this poet with all his in-equality, his rare beginnings and lame conclusions, his tedious moralisings and fine intuitions, his echoes and at the same time his new rendering of his tradition, unique. Certainly he is the poet of a few poems which among much that is mediocre shine as unforgettable and dateless. He reaches the fruit of his thought and the height of his art in such as ' The World,'[2] ' The Retreate,'[3] ' They are all gone into the world of light,'[4] and especially in a poem perfect of its kind, ' The Night.'[5] For ' The Night ' is a poem that, unlike many

---

[1] Blunden. *On the Poems of Henry Vaughan*, p. 41.
[2] Vaughan, II, 466.   [4] II, 483.
[3] II, 419.   [5] II, 522.

of Vaughan's poems which describe an epicyclic or zigzag course, develops on perfect curves of thought and image to its end, whether that end be viewed as climax, or as the completion of a symbolic circle with the image of returning to remain ' invisible and dim ' in the source which is for Vaughan the divine. The first stanza of ' The World ' and the last of ' The Night ' present together the two recurring images of the mystics—the circle of light, and, in the Dionysian phrase familiar to so many in Vaughan's age, the ' Ray of Darkness.'[1] But even among the remaining poems are numerous bright flashes, ' strange thoughts ' as Vaughan himself has said, transcending perhaps the theme they intend to illustrate. We name here, and reserve for further notice, the poems called ' Resurrection and Immortality,'[2] ' Vanity of Spirit,'[3] ' The Dawning,'[4] ' Man,'[5] ' Cock-crowing,'[6] ' The Bird,'[7] ' The Timber,'[8] and ' The Book.'[9] These, and others, become revelations when viewed in the light of some ideas that their writer harboured, and at the angle of his peculiar inner experience.

Vaughan wrote *Silex Scintillans* when the ' metaphysical ' fashion in poetry was ready to decline. His link with that fashion is sincere enough for it to have helped him to some of his best expressions, those wherein he is suddenly concentrated, and lucid with a simplicity with which metaphysical poets are not always lucid. He is essentially metaphysical in the wider sense of the word, when he expounds the ' sympathy ' that binds the natural world in one, when he interprets this sympathy as flowing from

---

[1] Dionysius the Areopagite. *De Mystice Theologia :* ' supernaturalis illius caliginis divinae radius ' (Migne, col. 999).

[2] II, 400.	[5] II, 477.	[8] II, 497.
[3] II, 418.	[6] II, 488.	[9] II, 540.
[4] II, 451.	[7] II, 496.	

a divine source, or lays bare his own longing to return to the source. But he has not the illuminating wit of the best of the metaphysical school ; he is, on the one hand, no ' priest of Apollo,'[1] and though, on the other, he often moralises, he has no grace in moralising like George Herbert ; he lacks Donne's or Marvell's irony ; he cannot clinch like Marvell with his splendid incisiveness tragic or gay, and his fine command of his subject ; for to clinch requires a certain quality of intellect, which is the faculty to see boundary-lines and definitions ; and Vaughan's real subject is often indefinable and so eludes his effort to present it. Many of his poems, like the lines on ' The Timber,' begin with vivid inspiration, which later dies and leaves the rest of the poem dull and forlorn, because the gleam has returned to its source in the subconscious, and Vaughan's conscious mind, which is not strong or subtle, cannot follow it. He feels too a sense of obscurity ; he is aware of falling short of perfect radiance in his spiritual life ; and in the poetry, itself less than fully articulate, he is constantly trying to express this sense. This again is the sign of a persistent groping towards some elusive memory, some half-forgotten happiness, which seldom swims into his clearer ken, but soothes him while it provokes with its promises of peace and delight—the pushing into flower again of his ' shootes of everlastingnesse,'[2] or the capacity to ' travell back '[3] to the ' early dayes '[4] and ' first, happy age '[5] which he dwells on in ' The Retreate ' and elsewhere. In ' Cock-crowing ' and in other poems he attempts to describe this sense of obscurity and half-defeat.

---

[1] See Carew's ' An Elegy upon the Death of Dr. Donne,' ll. 95–6.
[2] ' The Retreate,' II, 419.   [4] Ibid.
[3] Ibid.   [5] ' Looking Back,' II, 640.

Onely this Veyle which thou hast broke,
And must be broken yet in me,
This veyle, I say, is all the cloke
And cloud which shadows thee from me.
This veyle thy full-ey'd love denies,
And only gleams and fractions spies.[1]

But it may be said that with him as with other mystics the ' gleams and fractions ' are themselves responsible for the dimmer intervals which he experiences, as transient light outlines the dark ; and that when they occur he is able by their light to transcend the themes of other poets who are better artists.

[1] II, 488.

II

VAUGHAN has been viewed as a Nature-mystic, a mystic of the Anglican Church, and a platonic poet. He is not 'platonical' like Henry More, whose platonism, fantastic as the expression of it may appear in his verse, is a philosophical scheme arrived at by reasoning and synthesis. Vaughan, though he speculated much, did not much rationalise or formulate ; his thought is fused into image as it passes into consciousness ; and even that belief in the pre-existence of souls with which he has been credited,[1] is never openly declared. He is platonic in his continual conviction of an invisible presence behind or within the visible, and the peculiar presentation in his poetry of a natural world which is entirely sentient, and in contact with the sentient heart, not merely visible to the sensuous eye. His intercourse with this Nature alternates between conscious discipleship and a kind of unconscious interpenetration[2] of himself with a 'Spirit' which his special philosophy taught him to find in the objects of Nature, but which he could not have found had not some inner experience of his own sharpened his investigation. By means of this intercourse he describes not so much external Nature as the results of the interpenetration in terms of natural

[1] E.g. in *Les Doctrines Médiévales chez Donne*, by M. P. Ramsay (Oxford, 1917), p. 32 : ' Il adopte la thèse plotinienne de la préexistence dans le monde intelligible des âmes humaines.'

[2] In Shelley's use of the word. Compare the ' Lines written among the Euganean Hills.'

images. He heard the ' shrill '[1] voice of springs and
the ' whisper '[2] of leaves ; he saw the climbing or
falling mountain mists and the distant, kindling
light of stars ; but an inward voice was needed as
well to recollection, which when it spoke, spoke in
terms of Nature of a further and perhaps deeper reality.

> I . . . came at last
> To search my selfe, where I did find
> Traces, and sounds of a strange kind.
> Here of this mighty spring, I found some drills,
> With Ecchoes beaten from th'eternall hills ;[3]

This special experience awaits our discussion.
But it may be noted how different a poet of Nature he
is from the Nature-loving Marvell, who with a stronger
sense of objectivity, and a keen and admiring eye
for the ' endless variety ' of things, sees rather a
different earth from Vaughan's, and knows himself
as comrade of the creatures rather than disciple.
When Marvell imagines himself a tree, the process
and result are quite different from those when Vaughan
so imagines ; his witty grasshoppers perched on the
' unfathomable ' grass of Appleton meadow (' Where
Men like Grashoppers appear, But Grashoppers are
Gyants there,' and ' in there squeking Laugh, con-
temn Us as we walk more low then them ')[4] have
another outlook than Vaughan's devout and single-
hearted cock ;[5] and his flowers, ' Tulip Pinke and
Rose ' ' at parade,'[6] act quite otherwise from Vaughan's
hidden herbs and violets.[7] Even that wonderful

---

[1] ' Vanity of Spirit,' II, 418.
[2] ' Joy,' II, 491 ; ' Rules and Lessons,' II, 436.
[3] ' Vanity of Spirit,' II, 418.
[4] ' Upon Appleton House.' Marvell, I, 70.
[5] ' Cock-crowing,' II, 488.
[6] ' Upon Appleton House.' Marvell, I, 68.
[7] Compare, e.g., some references in the poems ' The Favour,' II, 492 ;
' The Seed growing secretly,' II, 510 ; ' Death,' II, 533.

B

passing vision, the ' Saphir-winged Mist ' of the
kingfisher in the twilight,[1] is more sensuous, more
independent, more superbly actual, than the creatures
of the Silurist's world. Or again, when as ' easie Philosopher ' Marvell ' confers ' among the birds and trees,
and delights in imagining man's metamorphosis—

> Give me but wings as they, and I
> Streight floting on the Air shall fly :
> Or turn me but, and you shall see
> I was but an inverted Tree.

—he is only accentuating the natural privilege of
that other bird, his mind, which can fly to ' other
Worlds ' and ' other Seas '[2] of its own creating ; and
even when he is ' Annihilating all that's made To a
green Thought in a green Shade '[3] he is taking the
tree's attributes into his securer possession.   Vaughan
in his own poem ' The Timber,' looking into the heart
of the dead wood that was once a tree, where now
' not so much as dreams of light may shine,' ' philo-
sophises ' by shifting his centre to that of the tree ;
and seems to lose himself in reverie of its former life
with the continual changes of sun and storm, and the
harbouring of the ' many light Hearts and Wings
Which now are dead.'[4] He recreates the tree's life,
and for a time he lives in it. Throughout the range
of imagery of his special, almost his single kind, he is
one of the most intimate of poets. To describe what
he is or what he would be, without taking conscious
thought he turns to Nature—

[1] ' Upon Appleton House.' Marvell, I, 80. Mr. G. Williamson in *The
Donne Tradition* (Harvard University Press, 1930), remarks on the ' artificial
character of Marvell's images of Nature ' (pp. 156–8). I think he is right ;
and yet feel at the same time the original and vigorous delight of Marvell
in the natural life surrounding him.

[2] ' The Garden.' Marvell, I, 49.

[3] Ibid.   [4] ' The Timber,' II, 497.

> The Blades of grasse, thy Creatures feeding,
> The trees, their leafs ; the flowres, their seeding ;
> The Dust, of which I am a part,
> The Stones much softer than my heart,
> The drops of rain, the sighs of wind,
> The Stars to which I am stark blind,
> The Dew thy herbs drink up by night,
> The beams they warm them at i' th' light. . . .[1]

For all these creatures can in some way represent him.

And yet, though he describes himself as Silurist,[2] and numerous poems image the scenery of lake and hill and river around him, he presents a Nature *sub specie æternitatis*, almost without a local habitation. The reader of his verses may indeed recognise fragments of an actual surrounding scene in the image of ' this hill ' ' drest ' in the ' faint beams ' remaining after sunset ;[3] or of ' That drowsie Lake ';[4] or ' This late, long heat ';[5] or of the streams appearing in *Silex Scintillans*, which, not belonging entirely to a world of symbols as do for instance Shelley's rivers, not fully actual like Wordsworth's Derwent and Yarrow, keep a middle nature between the imagined and the real, by virtue of which they become representative of the poet's inner life.

> as this restless, vocall Spring
> All day and night doth run, and sing,
> And though here born, yet is acquainted
> Elsewhere, and flowing keeps untainted. . . .[6]

They flow in the hills of Vaughan's native Brecon,

---

[1] ' Repentance,' II, 448–9.

[2] As a native of Brecknockshire, the country of the old Silures. ' You know that Silures contayned Breconockshire, Herefordshire, etc.' (*Aubrey's Brief Lives*, ed. A. Clark. Oxford, 1898. Vol. II, p. 269.)

[3] ' They are all gone into the world of light,' II, 483.

[4] ' The Showre,' II, 412.

[5] ' The Tempest,' II, 460.

[6] ' The Dawning,' II, 452.

but like the rest of Nature they are symbolic of ' Eden ' and the ' first estate.'

Again, his natural images are seen through the veil of his special desire. There are few clear open pictures, like those in Milton's cosmic landscape, of setting sun,[1] for instance, or moon rising in ' peerless light ';[2] or the series of scenes, clear as cameos, in *L'Allegro* and *Il Penseroso*. Here and there Vaughan has images which suggest the scenery of dreams, uncoloured and unappropriated.

> who stays
> Here long must passe
> O're dark hills, swift streames, and steep ways
> As smooth as glasse.[3]

He does not write of the world in terms of ' beauty,' like his contemporary and in some respects his fellow, Traherne, who sees all suffused with radiance, ' a mirror of infinite beauty,'[4] ' an illimited field of Variety and Beauty,'[5] and ' this little Cottage of heaven and Earth '[6] become the ' Palace '[7] of God, where man is not an outcast as with some writers in this seventeenth century, or an alien as with Vaughan, but the inheritor of the resplendent earth. Traherne loves the great ' creatures '—the sun ; the sea ; the air, ' a living miracle ' ;[8] the riches of the natural light. Vaughan broods on Nature in aspects of its sentience, and of a ' sympathy ' whose special connotation needs to be explained ; he dives into the heart of particular creatures ; he seeks to merge himself and be lost in the midst of the natural scene, as at the end of ' The Night ' he seeks to merge himself in the Divine ; and

---

[1] *P.L.*, IV, 591–7. [2] Ibid., 606–9.
[3] ' Joy of my life ! while left me here,' II, 423.
[4] Traherne, *Centuries*, p. 21. [7] Ibid., p. 20.
[5] Ibid., p. 12. [8] Ibid., p. 87.
[6] Ibid., p. 12.

often he is grieved because he cannot so be merged
and lost. At such times and in such moods he is that
universal poet whom Mrs. Meynell once analysed :

> Pines thy fallen nature ever
> For the unfallen Nature sweet.[1]

And when again the word ' fallen ' recalls us to
Vaughan's own century, to the other religious poets
and the theologians, to all the tops of speculation and
to the unfortunate *massa damnata* itself, we remember
that he has much to say of man as well as of the rest
of Nature, of man in exile, straying, and seeking to
return to a lost happiness whose symbol is ' Eden '[2]
or the ' early dayes.' Sometimes the objects of the
natural world retrieve this Eden,

> When on some *gilded Cloud*, or *flowre*
> My gazing soul would dwell an houre,
> And in those weaker glories spy
> Some shadows of eternity.[3]

Sometimes they too ' their heads lift, and expect '
redemption.[4] But in either case they continually
plead to Vaughan the recollection and ' retreat ' he
describes himself as seeking. Exiled as he was from
political interests by the defeat of the Royalist party,
and secluded in the quiet of his Welsh birthplace,
he found traces of his lost paradise among the Silurian
hills and streams. There too he experienced the
' conversion ' which set him on their track.

---

[1] Alice Meynell, ' To Any Poet,' *Poems*, p. 55.
[2] E.g., in ' Corruption,' II, 440.
[3] ' The Retreat,' II, 419.
[4] ' And do they so ? Have they a Sense ? ' II, 432.

III

WHAT happened between Vaughan's *Olor Iscanus* and
his *Silex Scintillans* ? Some experience, chiefly inward,
even if partly educed by outward events, made of a
dilettante in the metaphysical school the poet of ' The
Retreate,' ' The World,' and ' The Night,' and those
other poems where he meditates on the eternal aspects
of flowers, grass, trees, creatures, and men. Palinodes
were the fashion in the sixteenth and seventeenth
centuries ; and Vaughan, in the rather harsh preface
to his new book, repudiates his earlier verse. Conver-
sions were frequent, though less marked in the tradition
of the Anglican Church, in the line of Andrewes,
Donne, and Herbert, than among the ecstatic, comba-
tive sects. We perceive that between Donne's earlier
and later poetry there is no such bridge to be crossed
as with Vaughan ; divine and profane employ the same
symbols. And between Vaughan's conflict and that
of his master Herbert there is a difference to be noted,
and between their best poems a world of difference.
Vaughan claims for Herbert the credit of his ' conversion ' ; yet what he awakened to was not Herbert's
strenuous, punctual piety. Throughout *Silex Scintillans,*
consciously, or sometimes perhaps unconsciously,
he echoes Herbert's poetry. He comes forward to
answer the plea of Herbert's ' Obedience '[1] in his own
poem ' The Match.'[2] In ' Obedience ' Herbert offers
his poem as a ' deed ' to God ; and then, after ex-

[1] Herbert, II, 387.
[2] II, 434.

cluding certain possible claimants, such as Pleasure
or his own will, concludes

> He that will passe his land
> As I have mine, may set his hand
> And heart unto this deed, when he hath read,
> And make the purchase spread
> To both our goods, if he to it will stand.

> How happie were my part,
> If some kinde man would thrust his heart
> Into these lines ; till in heav'n's court of rolls
> They were by winged souls
> Entred for both, farre above their desert !

And Vaughan, addressing his own poem to Herbert,
the ' Dear friend ' whose ' holy, ever-living lines
Have done much good To many,' and among those
many to himself, comes forward to fulfil the wish.

> Here I joyn hands, and thrust my stubborn heart
> Into thy *Deed.*

And in truth he does make it possible that many lines
and phrases in *The Temple* shall be ' entred for both.'
Any careful reader of the two poets may well be
astonished at the devotion of this disciple and plagiarist,
and at the persistency of the echoes in *Silex Scintillans.*
Vaughan begs titles from Herbert, and while he draws
a title from one poem in *The Temple*, goes in debt to
another for images or phrases. Cross-correspondences
between a group of poems appear frequently ; and
frequently, too, not possessing Herbert's ready wit
or lyric finish, he appears as the borrower who does not
' better.' But the reader who will go further perceives
before long the deeper difference ; he finds him at
rarer moments transforming his borrowings, giving
them a new dress that quite alters their aspect ; or

finds him in those remoter places where Herbert
never came. Vaughan's traditions were those of the
Anglican Church, and he is outspokenly loyal ; but
his poetry confesses as well an older allegiance. His
devotion moreover towards the Church is crossed by
other elements—strange hieroglyphs, colours and
fragments of antiquity, alien to orthodox religion.
And he stresses revelations that orthodoxy had sometimes forgotten.

> No mercy-seat of gold,
> No dead and dusty *Cherub*, nor carv'd stone
> But his own living works did my Lord hold
> And lodge alone ;
> Where *trees* and *herbs* did watch and peep
> And wonder. . . .[1]

Even the Emblem to *Silex Scintillans*,[2] or the Dedica-
tion with its octosyllables pleading so naïvely against
' ev'ry publish'd vanity Which thou divinely hast
forgiven,'[3] are less closely characteristic than those
poems where, instead of the plea of sin and a divine
sacrifice—that which meant so much to Donne or
Herbert or Crashaw—he compares himself with herb
or star, bird or stone, creatures which have kept their
obligations ;[4] and looks for the atoning spirit which
shall repair the broken links in the creation.

To understand Vaughan's ' conversion,' and the
change between *Olor Iscanus* and *Silex Scintillans*, we
take the hints he gives us in his Preface to the latter—
the mention of an illness which brought him, he said,
' nigh unto death,'[5] and the tribute paid to Herbert,
with the claim of being ' the least ' among Herbert's
' pious *Converts*.'[6] To these we add the fact of his

---

[1] ' The Night,' II, 522.   [2] See p. 61.   [3] II, 395.
[4] ' Obligations ' in the literal sense. See account of ' sympathy ' *infra*.
[5] II, 392.   [6] II, 391.

seclusion in Scethrog, and his relations with his twin-brother Thomas, who, deprived of his clerical living by Cromwell's Independents, began or resumed the study of alchemy and of the Hermetic philosophy of Cornelius Agrippa. Thomas Vaughan, like his brother, was a curious reader. He knew something of the Rosicrucians, recent adventurers in 'occult' experience ; of the writings ascribed to the shadowy Trismegistus ; and of other Hermetic writers. He attempted metaphysical poetry himself, and like other metaphysical poets he knew the 'right-ey'd Areopagite,'[1] Dionysius. He knew Herbert too, well enough at any rate to travesty him ;[2] and gives evidence of some knowledge of the writings of Jacob Boehme. The brothers had been brought up together, they went to the same school and University, and for a few years at least they were both practising their several professions in Brecknockshire, Thomas as divine, Henry as physician. As with Robert Burton thirty years before, it would seem that with both brothers these interests crossed and mingled. Both, too, explored the natural world in search of hidden meanings. Even when Thomas Vaughan left Brecon and pursued his studies of alchemy in Oxford and London, the brothers must have been in contact, and contact, it seems, of an intimate kind ; for then it is that the closest outward correspondence occurs, in various parallel phrases and images which appear in *Silex Scintillans* and in some of Thomas Vaughan's treatises. Like *Silex*

[1] Crashaw, ed. Martin, p. 259, ' The Epiphanie of our Lord.'

[2] In *Anima Magica Abscondita* (p. 47) he adapts a stanza of Herbert's ' Gratefulnesse ' (Herbert, III, 43). He describes the true ' magician's ' preparations for the entrance of the divine spirit into matter. ' Thou must *tyre* him out with *pious importunities*.

> *Perpetuall knockings at his Doore,*
> *Teares sullying his transparent Roomes,*
> *Sighes upon sighes : weep more and more,*
> *He comes.'*

Scintillans, several of these treatises were published in 1650.

We do not know when Henry Vaughan, poet and physician, first came in contact with these Hermetic traditions, which to poetry as to medicine proposed fresh fields. He may have known them since his Oxford days, though there is nothing indicative of his later deep apprehension of them in *Olor Iscanus*. Their influence, like the influence of Herbert, may have reached him at the time of his ' conversion,' this particular time when he was more than ordinarily impressionable ; and revived or sharpened latent powers of intuition. His rendering of the traditions is unique ; it is different from the reading his brother gives in those treatises of approved Hermetic nomenclature—*Anima Magica Abscondita*, *Anthroposophia Theomagia*, *Magia Adamica*, *Lumen de Lumine*, and others—different even in the midst of the striking resemblance we have mentioned, and which will presently be illustrated. Henry's interpretation is finer, less credulous perhaps on some points, but more religious ; and here again not only because the Hermetic tradition met the Catholic, and deepened it, and was in its turn refined ; but also because between them and enriching both lies some individual experience of the poet.

This experience was, as we have suggested, rather a ' recollection ' than a conversion. Yet psychologically much conversion is of the nature of recollection ; it is an upheaval of the subconscious into consciousness, under pressure of supreme emotion, or at a time when the ordinary bodily claims are weakened. One who had been, as Vaughan says of himself, ' nigh unto death ' would be peculiarly liable ; and many persons, though perhaps in lesser degree, may have felt a conviction of a revival that has seemed spiritual as well as physical, almost the sense of a ' re-birth,' in the first days of convalescence. We can know that Vaughan's nature was subject to such impressions ; for he could experience an ordinary awakening from sleep as a kind of re-birth (here again perhaps the experience is common), and feel that in sleep some process of purification, of re-integration at a primal source, had been at work upon him.

> with what flowres,
> And shoots of glory, my soul breakes, and buds !
> All the long houres
> Of night, and Rest
> Through the still shrouds
> Of sleep, and Clouds,
> This Dew fell on my Breast ;[1]

In the same poem this sense of recreation leads to the sense of a common consciousness with Nature ; and may it not have been that, secluded in Scethrog from the world of society and action, and still further withdrawn by a severe illness, Vaughan read Herbert's poetry and read or re-read some Hermetic books, and descending into his own mind, saw or thought he saw a glimpse of the origins of creation, and of what he calls in one of his poems the ' tye of Bodyes,'[2] inaugurating thereby a desire which was to haunt him all the remainder of his life ? Readers of W. H. Hudson's books will remember the experience described in *Far Away and Long Ago*, where the writer tells how in recovering from a long illness he saw all his childhood spread out in memory before him.[3] Readers of Blake will remember how (and this too is the account of an experience which a temperament like Blake's might undergo repeatedly)

---

[1] ' The Morning-Watch,' II, 424.
[2] ' Sure, there's a tye of Bodyes ! ' II, 429.
[3] Hudson. Chapter I, pp. 3-4.

I remain'd as a child ;
All I ever had known
Before me bright shone :[1]

Between Vaughan's outlook and Hudson's there are
some close analogies. Both possess an intuition by
which they ' see into the life of things.'[2] And in his
chapter called ' A Boy's Animism ' Hudson describes
' this sense ' he had ' of the supernatural in natural
things.'[3] He experiences a magical influence from
trees, and feels too that some trees in particular are
' intensely alive,' although this peculiar effect is felt
' not only in moonlit trees or in a flower or serpent,
but in certain exquisite moments and moods and in
certain aspects of nature, in " every grass " and in all
things, animate and inanimate.'[4] The reader of Henry
Vaughan has only to turn to such poems as ' The
Bird,'[5] ' The Timber,'[6] or ' The Book '[7] to discover
how closely this account could fit the seventeenth-
century worshipper of Nature. Vaughan also, for all
the self-accusations found in some poems, possessed
with Blake the simplicity and candour of heart which
made them each the lover of children and of humble
creatures, of morning and purity and the springing
resilient life of earth.

Both Christian and Hermetic teaching reiterate
' Ye must be born again '[8] . . . ' become as little
children.' The upheaval of the subconscious mind

[1] ' To Thomas Butts,' Blake, ed. Sampson, p. 186.
[2] Wordsworth, *Tintern Abbey.*
[3] Hudson, op. cit., p. 226.
[4] Ibid., pp. 231–33.
[5] II, 496.   [6] II, 497.   [7] II, 540.
[8] St. John, III, 7. (The Greek is γεννηθῆναι ἄνωθεν ; but the significance
remains the same.) With this N.T. passage compare the discourse of ' Hermes
Trismegistus to his son Tat, concerning Rebirth ' (*Hermetica,* vol. I, p. 239) :
'. . . You said that no one can be saved until he has been born again, . . . I
know not, thrice-greatest one, from what womb a·man can be born again,
nor from what seed.'

may mean the uncovering of those lowest layers of memory which record the experiences of pre-natal life. Such a glimpse would seem to the experient to reveal the unity underlying all the life of Nature, and the essential affinity between man and the rest of Nature (this is the origin and significance of the state known as ' cosmic consciousness ') ; and might, as we think possible in Vaughan's case, haunt him for ever after with a conviction of exile from a once-known peace and purity, and a vague apprehension of some mysterious beauty which would seem to him to have had no beginning in time—the ' Something I can never find, Something lying on the ground, In the bottom of my mind '[1] according to one modern poet, or ' The flagstone under all, the fire of fires, The roots of the world '[2] of another. To Vaughan, in the seventeenth century, and in the midst of speculation theological, Platonic, and Hermetical, the symbol is ' Eden ' ; or the ' early days ' ; or the ' first, happy age ' ; or perhaps the patriarchs, ' those first white Pilgrims,'[3] who in many poems are typical,[4] since they, like the subject of ' The Retreate,' had not yet walked ' Above a mile or two ' from Eden ; or (as we shall presently see) any of those symbols of the alchemists which are designed to denote the utmost perfection in Nature. Or again, the symbol is morning, childhood, whiteness, in its aspects of refreshment ; or ' the wombe of things,'[5] the ' mothers bosome,'[6] night, the ' eternal hills,' in its aspects of untroubled and self-forgetting peace. Even perhaps it is the ' deep but dazling darkness ' of God, where, weary of the sun which here symbolises the world, he might ' live invisible and dim.'[7]

---

[1] James Stephens, ' The Goat Paths.'
[2] W. B. Yeats, *The Shadowy Waters.*
[3] ' The day of Judgement,' II, 531.
[4] See, e.g., ' Corruption,' II, 440.
[5] ' Resurrection and Immortality,' II, 401.
[6] ' Death,' II, 400.
[7] ' The Night,' II, 523.

I . . . came at last
To search my selfe, where I did find
Traces, and sounds of a strange kind.
Here of this mighty spring, I found some drills,
With Ecchoes beaten from th'eternall hills.[1]

Others in this seventeenth century when they ' came
to search themselves ' might find, at different levels
of their minds, rather different elements. Donne could
at one time find ' Despair behind, and death before,'[2]
or, again, the mingled fear and fascination which
the thought of death could bring alternating with
flights of a troubled joy, and an overwhelming impression of divine transcendence. Herbert found the cease-
less fluctuations of hope and anxiety in a soul more
sensitive than strong. Bunyan saw personal terror,
and afterwards sheer relief ; as George Fox saw both
terror and love projected over the world in his vision
of the oceans of darkness and light.[3] Jacob Boehme
told how, searching his own spirit, he saw ' the Eye
which is God,' ' the Natureless creatureless Deity . . .
Who also in himself willeth no more but only to find
and comprehend himself, and to go forth from himself,'
and so to create ' time, and Eternity ; Heaven, Hell ;
the world, light, and darkness ; paine, and *Source* ;
life, and death ; Something and Nothing.'[4] Boehme
deliberately strove to reach the beginning, the ' without
form,' the abyss seen in glimpses by those whose
nature impels them to penetrate the depths of the
subconscious ; and the symbolisation of what he saw
affords the content of most of what he wrote, while
he attempted to depict the agonies of generation in

[1] ' Vanity of Spirit,' II, 418.

[2] *Holy Sonnets*, I. Donne, *Poems*, ed. Grierson, I, 322.

[3] Fox, *Journal*, p. 13. ' I saw also, that there was an *Ocean* of *Darkness* and
Death ; but an infinite *Ocean* of *Light* and *Love*, which flowed over the *Ocean*
of *Darkness*.'

[4] Boehme, *XL Questions*, p. 42.

the divine or human spirit. Vaughan's younger con-
temporary Traherne tells of a realisation akin to
Vaughan's own ; for—without dwelling at all on that
factor of ' death unto sin ' which Herbert's convert
could not altogether leave out—Traherne flies straight
to his mark, and writes of the recollection of and
return to a state of happiness and purity known during
the first years of life, and between which and the
later realisation had fallen, as he describes it in the
Centuries of Meditations, a time of spiritual dulness and
distraction. In both prose and poetry he depicts such
a state as Vaughan images after a different fashion in
' The Retreate ' ; but whereas Vaughan, feeling himself alienated, longs to ' travell back,' Traherne claims
to have attained again and to enjoy. He seems to be
writing from some later radiant conviction, and seeing
the early days enhanced in its light. The state which in
the poems he tries to describe is one of learning yet of
possession, something belonging to childhood yet
deeper than a child's first conscious knowledge.
Sometimes it appears as even earlier in time than the
limpid intercourse suggested by

> He in our childhood with us walks,
> And with our thoughts mysteriously He talks.[1]

for in ' The Praeparative,'[2] it is that of ' My Body being
dead, my Limbs unknown ' ; or in another part of the
same poem that of

> an inward Sphere of Light...
> All Life, all Sense,
> A naked, simple, pure intelligence.

Such a description, or that of the sense of ' naked,
simple Life '[3] in another poem, a sense so strong that

---

[1] ' The Approach,' Traherne, *Poems,* p. 69.
[2] Ibid. *Poems,* p. 13.   [3] ' My Spirit.' Ibid. *Poems,* p. 73.

the act of perception and the thing perceived merge in ' the Substance of the mind,' may remind the reader of some of Wordsworth's poignant solitary moods. Here, however, it seems to point to a belief in the writer in the pre-existence of human souls. It resembles too Henry More's doctrine of the soul revolving on itself and reflecting, and able to ' uncase ' matter ' of all her forms,' and discover ' a nak'd simple essence.'[1] The soul in More is ' tri-central,' with its highest part awake perhaps from eternity ; but all three parts are pre-existent. In Thomas Vaughan's philosophy also the souls have ' an Explicite Methodicall knowledge ' ' before their Intrance into the body.'[2] Henry Vaughan, though he writes in ' The Retreate ' of a ' second race,'[3] and in ' The Waterfall ' of human souls as coming from ' a sea of light,'[4] never declares in positive phrase a belief in pre-existence. With him it is the return to source that is stressed—the ' backward steps ' ;[5] the ' love turn'd retrograde,'[6] as his own expressive English renders one of the metres of Boethius, giving it his own inflection of thought.

To Traherne as to Vaughan childhood is a state of candid and undisturbed purity,

> Ev'n like the Streams of Crystal Springs,
> Where all the curious things
> Do from the bottom of the Well appear.[7]

The ' curious things ' at ' the bottom of the well ' recall Vaughan's ' strange sounds ' and ' traces '[8] when he came to search himself ; or that recollection of the ' eternal mind ' which haunts the child in

---

[1] More, *Psychathanasia*, p. 53.
[2] T. Vaughan, *Anthroposophia Theomagia*, p. 2.
[3] II, 419.
[4] II, 527.
[5] ' The Retreate,' II, 420.
[6] II, 633.
[7] ' The World,' Traherne, *Poems*, p. 26.
[8] ' Vanity of Spirit,' II, 418.

Wordsworth's *Ode*.[1] ' Childhood,' writes Traherne,

> might itself alone be said
> My Tutor, teacher, Guide to be ;
> Ev'n then Instructed by the Deity.[2]

or, again, in another poem,

> To Infancy, O Lord, again I com,
> That I my Manhood may improv :
> My early Tutor is the Womb.[3]

And we notice a passage in Boehme's *XL Questions Concerning the Soule* which is of interest to us here, and arresting in an age which believed with Donne and Augustine that ' as soon as wee are any thing, wee are sinners, and there, where there can be no more tentation ministered to us, than was to the Angels, that fell in heaven, that is, in *our mothers wombe*.'[4] Boehme writes

> Little children are our Schoolmasters till evill stirre in them . . . they bring their sport from the Mothers wombe, which is a Remnant of Paradise : but all the rest is gone till we shall receive it againe.[5]

The coincidence with Traherne's poetry is striking. Perhaps the latter, who was widely read, a student of Plato and Plotinus, and also of Pico della Mirandola,[6] had found out Jacob Boehme, whose writings had just become accessible in the translations of John Sparrow. Thomas Vaughan knew Boehme's *The Three Principles* at least, and praises it in a note to his own *Magia Adamica* ;[7] and we may think it probable, though we have no proof, that Henry, with his love

---

[1] Wordsworth, ' Ode on Intimations of Immortality.'
[2] ' The Approach,' Traherne, *Poems*, p. 70.
[3] ' The Return,' Ibid., p. 12.
[4] Donne, *Fifty Sermons*, p. 187.
[5] Boehme, *XL Questions*, p. 130.
[6] Compare the *Centuries*, p. 298.
[7] T. Vaughan, *Magia Adamica*, p. 110 (note).

c

of the curious, his taste for speculation, and the close correspondence which (as we shall further show) exists between the writings of the brothers, read too in Boehme's voluminous and deep though not many-sided treatises. Ideas, however, are in the air at certain periods ; there are, as Dr. Denis Saurat has pointed out, ' zones ' of ideas ;[1] and within these zones, as within zones of infection, certain spirits are peculiarly susceptible. Many epidemic ideas visited the seventeenth century ; and Plato and Plotinus were studied by select thinkers, and Pico had brought the Cabbala into wider repute. Writers and thinkers do not always take the infection direct from each other ; they yield perhaps to the surrounding influence. We do not know why Vaughan and Traherne both expressed themselves as desiring to ' travell back,' nor why this special awareness is felt in English poetry for the first time here. But in connection with Boehme we remember that Vaughan too when he gazed at childhood thought

> How do I study now, and scan
> Thee, more than ere I studyed man.[2]

and longed by studying to learn to ' retreat,' although, as he tells us, he seems to himself to be looking through a ' long night ' at the ' edges ' and ' bordering light ' only of that strange and happy time.

Again, his sense of affinity with herb and flower, and even with dust and stones, may have been developed in some such subconscious process as we have tried to indicate. For he not only believed with the Hermetists in the ' tye of bodies,'[3] but he felt the tie ; and the expression of his sense of kinship with

---

[1] D. Saurat, *Literature and Occult Tradition*, trans. D. Bolton (London, 1930), pp. 59–60.
[2] ' Childe-hood,' II, 521.
[3] ' Sure, there's a tye of Bodyes !' II, 429.

the creatures of Nature leaves a curious impression in the reader's mind of a tie strong as the physical or even the uterine link, forged before consciousness in ' the wombe of things.'[1] The poetry embodying this half-conscious desire for unity and re-absorption has much of the quality known as ' atmosphere '; it retains if not memories at least what Matthew Arnold calls ' murmurs and scents.' It gives a different impression from that which Traherne's poetry gives, and quite different from the effect of More's philosophical poetry, different too once more from the effect gained in reading that fantastic, credulous spirit, his own brother. Henry Vaughan is more reserved, more sensitive, and at the same time more deeply involved.

---

[1] Vaughan, ' Resurrection and Immortality,' II, 401.

IV

But linked with this sense of affinity and sympathy
we meet with a definite tradition and technology, and
must proceed to quote and explain a few terms from the
Hermetic or ' occult ' philosophy, since only through
an understanding of some such terms and symbols
can Henry Vaughan's poetry and faith be fully appre-
ciated. We need in this place quote no more than those
which serve this purpose.

The Hermetic philosophy, with its traditional
beginnings lodged not only with Moses or the mythical
Hermes Trismegistus, but referred back by some of
its adherents to Seth, Enoch, Adam, or even to the
lapsed angels of the story in the sixth chapter of
Genesis, was probably of Chaldæan origin, but was
closely akin at some points to the traditions of the
Jewish Cabbala ; gave hints to Pythagoras, and to
Plato in the *Timaeus ;* and embodied much of itself
in Gnosticism. Later it reached mediaeval Europe
through its Arabian practicians and exponents, and
was revived as a field for inquiry and mystic speculation after the Renaissance, while its ancient sciences
of astrology and alchemy continued uninterruptedly
from its Chaldæan and Egyptian days. As a philosophy
it appears in the work of Post-Renaissance scholars
such as Pico della Mirandola ; and inspires the *De
Occulta Philosophia* of Cornelius Agrippa, and the
strange collection ascribed to Paracelsus. Many lesser
investigators, of varying degrees of learning, practical
sagacity, credulity and mysticism, are engaged on it,

like those whose writings appear in a volume styled *The Hermetic Museum,* which was published at Frankfort in 1648. Such an investigator was Thomas Vaughan, who when forced from his clerical living after the Independent victory began writing under the pseudonym of Eugenius Philalethes on a subject which had perhaps interested him for long. He acknowledges his debt to Agrippa, to whom ' next to God I owe all that I have '[1] (and though, as in the case of Boehme, we cannot prove that Henry Vaughan read Agrippa, we shall have to show there too some curious analogies) ; and rejects the ' Peripatetickes,' who ' look on *God,* as they do on *Carpenters,* who build with *Stone* and *Timber,* without any *infusion* of *life.* But the world, which is God's building, is full of *Spirit, quick,* and *living.*'[2] So, after their different ways, the world appears to Agrippa and Paracelsus, Jacob Boehme and Henry Vaughan. The ' elves of hills, brooks, standing lakes, and groves' are verities to Agrippa and Paracelsus,[3] and it is not difficult to ' start a spirit.'

The Hermetic doctrines were of a nature to appeal to that special kind of mediaevalism which lingered on in Europe till past the first half of the seventeenth century. As pure luxury of speculation they would attract such ' extravagant and irregular heads '[4] as those of Sir Thomas Browne or certain metaphysical poets. The metaphysical poets indeed, in their hope to track the quintessential beauty whether abstract or embodied, are first cousins to the alchemists. Milton amidst his wide classic knowledge knew the Cabbala well ; and he too, for all his rational, liberal tendencies, presents in *Paradise Lost* a scheme having

[1] T. Vaughan, *Anthroposophia Theomagia,* p. 50.   [2] Ibid., Sig. B3b.
[3] Compare Paracelsus (ed. Waite), vol. II, p. 269. ' There are many worlds : and we are not the only beings in our own world. . . . We are not the only beings made ; there were many more whom we do not know.'
[4] Browne, *Religio Medici,* p. 12.

features in common with the scheme of the Gnostics.[1]
The studies also of natural science and of medicine
were implicated with Hermetic theories, dangerous
and unsuitable as these had been considered by the
orthodox in religion and science. Henry Vaughan
writes that ' the most serious of our profession ' (the
profession which he shares with Browne and that
' famous and faithfull Chymist, Henry Nollius,'[2]
whose work he translated) ' have not only an unkind-
ness for, but are persecutors of Astrologie.'[3] Yet on
the other hand the Hermetists themselves are careful
not only to defend their practice from the charge of
necromancy, but generally to profess religious orthodoxy. It is against the Galenists rather than the
Catholics that Paracelsus protests ; and Agrippa,
though he like Paracelsus was regarded as a dangerous
magician, sums up the points of the Catholic creed in
the third book of his *Occult Philosophy*. Many minor
Hermetists make allegory of their alchemy, explaining
their ' mystery ' in terms of the Christian mystery, as
on a larger scale Jacob Boehme images the ' three
principles of the divine essence,'[4] and the ' threefold
life of man '[5] in terms of the chemical trinity of sulphur,
mercury, and salt. Sometimes the work of the ' tincture ' is made to represent the work of redemption, as
Donne uses it in his poem of ' Resurrection, imperfect.'

> Hee was all gold when he lay downe, but rose
> All tincture, and doth not alone dispose
> Leaden and iron wills to good, but is
> Of power to make even sinfull flesh like his.[6]

[1] Compare the account of this in *Milton, Man and Thinker*, by Denis
Saurat (London, 1925).
[2] Title-page to the translation of *Hermetical Physick*, Vaughan, II, 547.
[3] Letter to Aubrey. Vaughan, II, 672.
[4] Boehme, *The Three Principles of the Divine Essence*. English edition, 1648.
[5] Ibid., *The Threefold Life of Man*. English edition, 1650.
[6] Donne, *Poems*, I, 334.

And in one of Thomas Vaughan's treatises—an example among many such in this writer—two of the secret symbols of alchemy, Dragon and Serpent (sulphur and mercury), are converted to the use of Christian allegory. Satan is the false serpent tempting to the forbidden tree and the spurious title of godhead. ' But 'tis not this *subtill* Dragon, but *Bonus ille Serpens*, that *good*, *Crucified Serpent*, that can give us both this *Knowledge*, and this *Title*.'[1] Again the reader is reminded of the tone of metaphor in Donne's sermons ; and here, in fact, there is an actual parallel. Donne speaks of ' this Serpent, this creeping Serpent,' and of ' the other Serpent, the crucified Serpent ' in one of the *Fifty Sermons*. ' That creeping Serpent, Satan, is war, and should be so ; the crucified Serpent Christ Jesus is peace, and shall be so for ever. The creeping Serpent eats our dust, the strength of our bodies, in sicknesses, and our glory in dust, the dust of the grave : The crucified Serpent hath taken our flesh, and our blood, and given us his flesh, and his blood for it.'[2] The religious, mystery-loving century brought its religion and its magic into closer touch, and some refinement of material has taken place between the ' occult ' work of Paracelsus and that of Thomas Vaughan. Vaughan the poet, as we have remarked, refines still further, and when he would go ' in a thought ' ' To heav'n, or Earth below To reade some *Starre*, or Min'rall,'[3] takes only the light and winged part of the philosophy.

Agrippa writes in one place of how the mind,

[1] T. Vaughan, *Magia Adamica*, p. 40. It may be noticed in passing that one of the ancient indictments against alchemy presented it as tempting pre-eminently to forbidden knowledge.

[2] Donne, *Fifty Sermons*, p. 445.

[3] ' Resurrection and Immortality,' II, 402. Compare T. Vaughan, *Anthroposophia Theomagia*, p. 46 : ' She ' (the soul) ' spans kingdoms in a Thought.'

lifting itself up, can search all the ' stations, grounds,
causes and sciences of things,' and behold them ' as
it were in a certain glass of Eternity (*tanquam in quodam
aeternitati specula*).[1] Vaughan tells in one poem how
he was shown in ' a strange glass '

> That busie commerce kept between
> God and his Creatures, though unseen.[2]

And this is his special standpoint, and the substance
of much of his religion. His ' glass ' is unique because
the ' commerce ' is so intimate that it reveals, and
because rays from the Hermetic and the Catholic teaching meet at the angle of his inner experience.   But the
very need to search himself while he searches Nature,
though in his case an emotional need and the outcome
of converging impulses and resulting in individual
discoveries, has its parallel in the inculcations of
Hermetic teaching, which at its most consistent and
philosophical has much to say of the penetrative power
of man's mind. For man, entering into himself, shall
inherit all the earth. ' Whosoever therefore shall know
himself, shall know all things in himself ; especially
he shall know God, according to whose Image he was
made ; he shall know the world, the resemblance of
which he beareth ; he shall know all creatures, with
which he symboliseth ; and what comfort he can have
and obtain, from Stones, Plants, Animals, elements,
Heavens, from Spirits (*a demonibus*), Angels, and every
thing.'[3] Agrippa's ' fomentum ' suggests almost a
physical ' comfort,' like Vaughan's ' tye of Bodyes.'
And the latter's deep sympathy with Nature has its
parallel again in the theoretic ' sympathy ' of the
Hermetists, which again in its turn springs from another theory, a central theory in occult beliefs, the

---

[1] Agrippa, *Occult Philosophy*, trans. J.F., p. 367.
[2] ' The Stone,' II, 514.   [3] Agrippa, p. 460.

starting-point for the philosophy of Agrippa and the practice of Paracelsus, but an item of scholastic philosophy before their day.

' He shall know the world, the resemblance of which he beareth.' The theory of the microcosm and the macrocosm—that man, the ' little world,' includes all parts and elements of the greater world—permeated literature, and by no means only Hermetic or scholastic literature, of the sixteenth and seventeenth centuries. It agreed with the idealistic temper of the age as well as with the passion for ' ratiocination ' and spiritual diagram which was a scholastic legacy. As George Herbert puts it,

> Man is all symmetrie,
> Full of proportions, one limbe to another,
> And all to all the world besides.
> Each part may call the farthest, brother ;
> For hand with foot hath private amitie,
> And both with moons and tides.[1]

' This body is an illustration of all Nature '[2] says Donne too in one of his sermons, and in his rapt preoccupied fashion, he illustrates the cosmos from his own body in the *Devotions*[3] he wrote during an illness. The theory was presented popularly in crude physical diagram in the astrologers' almanacs, where the parts and organs of man's body were mapped out under the seven planets and twelve signs ; it was worked out in similar if more scientific fashion in the second book of Agrippa's *Occult Philosophy* ; yet its farthest implications were mystical. Valentine Weigel sets forth these results with comparative simplicity in the little treatise of *Astrologie Theologised*, which was published in England in 1649.

[1] ' Man.' Herbert, II, 217.   [2] Donne, *LXXX Sermons*, p. 823.
[3] *Devotions*, ed. J. Sparrow, Cambridge, 1923.

The *subject of Astrologie* therefore is double ; the Macrocosm and Microcosm, the greater World, and the lesser
World.[1]

Both these worlds are ' twofold ' ; ' visible according
to the body, invisible according to the soule or spirit.'[2]

Man, as to his body, is composed of the Elements, and as to
his soul, of the Starrs.[3]

Whatsoever is without a man, the same is also within
him . . . although the Macrocosme is without us, yet neverthe-
less it may also be found truly within us.[4]

Nor are we, nor do wee inhabit, walk and live in anything
els, save in that whereof we are made.[5]

So God is whole without us, and also whole within us.
. . . We have God every where with us, whether we know it,
or know it not.[6]

Weigel as a mystic draws the idea out to its full conclusions. So Jacob Boehme writes : ' *If* this whole or
universal Beeing, bee not God, *then* thou art not Gods
Image : If he be any other or strange God, then thou
hast *no part* in him : For thou art created out of this
God, and livest *in* this very God . . . also all thy
knowledge standeth in this God, and when thou
dyest, then thou art *Buried* in this God . . . How
shall that strange God, out of whom thou art *not*
created, and in whom thou didst *never* Live, bring
thy Body and Spirit *together again* ? '[7]

Vaughan has not much to say directly of microcosm
and macrocosm, though in ' Affliction ' he claims that
God displays in his ' greater world ' what he ' would do'
in the ' lesser,' man ;[8] and in ' Man's fall, and Recovery '
he makes the individual typical of the race, blending
his own experience with that of Adam, the prototype

[1] Weigel, p. 5.   [4] Ibid., p. 7.   [7] Boehme, *Aurora,* p.
[2] Ibid., p. 5.   [5] Ibid., p. 8.   539.
[3] Ibid., p. 6.   [6] Ibid., p. 8.   [8] II, 459.

and the first microcosm.[1] In another poem, imaging
some of Nature's events, he shows how all Nature can
be an illustration of man. ' How is man parcell'd out ?
how ev'ry hour Shows him himself.'[2] And throughout
his poetry the changes in the natural scene become
symbols of man's chequered inward life—' This
late, long heat ' ;[3] or the moisture from the mountain
lake which like the poet's own too slothful prayer is
unable to reach heaven, and can only descend in rain
and weep for its ' mistake ';[4] or the ' rainy, weeping
day ' which resembles man's whole life on earth.[5]
But when he would be more technical in phraseology
he writes of the ' inclosed Spirit ' which inhabits some
creatures (in this poem, ' hills and valleys, birds, and
poor stones '), and is to each ' a star Inlightning his
own little sphaere.'[6] This is in strict accordance with
Hermetic doctrine ; for the microcosm had its ' stars '
corresponding to the stars of the macrocosm, and in
its threefold life it possessed a ' sydereal spirit ' which
corresponded to the celestial or starry sphere of the
macrocosm. The greater and lesser worlds corresponded both in outline and in detail—in outline
because each was threefold, the universe being intellectual or angelic, celestial or starry, and terrestrial
or elementary, and the man composed of an ' ele-
mented ' body, an immortal soul, and a sydereal spirit
which acted as medium between soul and body ; in
detail because all the parts and elements of the macrocosm were comprised (virtually, not materially) in
man. This correspondence, with the ' sympathy ' it
involves, is the secret of the Hermetic medicine.
' Herbs gladly cure our flesh, because that they Find
their acquaintance there.' [7]

[1] II. 411.
[2] ' The Tempest,' II, 460.
[3] Ibid.
[4] ' The Showre,' II, 412.
[5] ' The Timber,' II, 498.
[6] ' The Bird,' II, 497.
[7] Herbert, ' Man,' II, 219.

God too, as Weigel and Boehme maintain, is
' whole within us.' Or at least there is a divine spark,
like the ' synteresis ' of some older writers among the
mystics. Closely allied with the synteresis in nature,
though considered scientifically as well as spiritually,
is the ' quintessence ' of the Hermetists, that fine and
pure and hidden essence which preserves each creature
from corruption, ' a matter most subtly purged of all
impurities and mortality.'[1] It is not, as Agrippa tells
us, generated ' from the four Elements, but a certain
first thing, having its being above, and besides them.'[2]
It appears as something on the boundary-line between
matter and spirit ; it also sums up in little the whole
creation and the whole world. Thus the earth from
which Adam, the first microcosm, was made was
' a meer quintessence, extracted from every part,
from the whole frame of the whole world.'[3] We are
back again with the microcosm and the macrocosm ;
and indeed many of the terms of this philosophy
resolve themselves out as various aspects of one elusive
ideal quantity, which to philosophers and practicians
seemed to hold the secret of life ; and which we to-day
might relate to the theory of the germ-plasm.

In man the quintessence is the link between soul
and body ; ' that spirit lives and moves in all elementary creatures, and is the indissoluble bond of body
and soul, the purest and most noble essence in which
lie hid all mysteries in their inexhaustible fulness of
marvellous virtue and efficacy.'[4] Similarly, in the
universe the quintessence draws the Soul of the
World[5] from the higher to the lower sphere. For as
the Catholics, from Aquinas to many minor mediaeval

[1] Paracelsus, ed. Waite, vol. II, p. 22.   [2] Agrippa, p. 33.
[3] Weigel, p. 19. With ' meer ' compare Lat. *merus.*
[4] *The Sophic Hydrolith. Hermetic Museum*, I, 78.
[5] The third principle of the Divine Being, as in the Gnostic and Plotinian
theories.

writers, saw the creation as a ' ladder ' or ' scale '
reaching through various rungs of being to the throne
of God, the mystic and Hermetic philosophers, from
Plotinus to the workers and explorers of Vaughan's
own day, saw the living Spirit stoop descending
through all things to inform them and link them
together—the descent which Thomas Vaughan describes in image as ' that most secret and silent Laps
of the *Spirit per Formarum naturalium Seriem.*'[1] This
Spirit, which the same writer in his treatise *Lumen de
Lumine* calls the ' *Light* of *Nature,*'[2] is in another
figure the ' secret *Candle* of *God,*' which hee hath
tinn'd in the *Elements,*' to which ' Every naturall
Body is a kind of *Black Lanthorne.*'[3]

When in his poem ' Resurrection and Immortality '
Henry Vaughan describes how ' a preserving spirit
doth still passe Untainted through this Masse '[4]
(i.e., this mass of corporal Nature), he refers to this
unifying and cleansing spirit, or quintessence, or
' tincture.' And in ' The Sap,' like Donne and others,
he figures Christ's redemption and sacrament under
this symbol in all its implications.

> To shew what strange love he had to our good,
>   He gave his sacred bloud,
> By wil our sap, and Cordial ; now in this
>   Lies such a heav'n of bliss,
> That, who but truly tasts it, no decay
>   Can touch him any way,
> Such secret life and vertue in it lies,
>   It wil exalt and rise
> And actuate such spirits as are shed
>   Or ready to be dead. . . .[5]

The ' tincture,' again, is an essence of kindred nature

---

[1] T. Vaughan, *Anthroposophia Theomagia*, p. 45.
[2] Ibid., *Lumen de Lumine*, p. 41.
[3] Ibid., p. 41.
[4] II, 401.
[5] II, 475.

to the quintessence, claimed by the alchemists to be
reached in their last process, and of itself ' a thing that
separateth, and bringeth the pure and cleere, from
the impure : and that bringeth the life of all sorts of
Spirits, or all sorts of Essences, into its highest . . .
degree. . . . Yea it is the cause of the shining, or of
the lustre : it is a cause that all creatures see and live.'[1]
So, in the opening of Vaughan's ' Repentance '—

> Lord, since thou didst in this vile Clay
> That sacred Ray
> Thy spirit plant, quickning the whole
> With that one grains infused wealth[2]

—the ' grain ' is a spiritual ' tincture,' imaged as light,
as Boehme images it in the passage just quoted.
And by this ' tincture,' this ' little grain ' that ' shines
and sings,' the cock in ' Cock-crowing ' is impelled
to await and greet the first ray of the sun.

> Their eyes watch for the morning hue,
> Their little grain expelling night
> So shines and sings, as if it knew
> The path unto the house of light.
> It seems their candle, howe'r done,
> Was tinn'd and lighted at the sunne.[3]

And night, to use again Boehme's image, is the ' impure ' mass which the ' pure and cleere ' light resolves.

More than any poem in *Silex Scintillans*, ' Cock-
crowing ' is steeped in Hermetic tradition and then
sublimated. Vaughan has caught his brother's figure
of the ' *Candle . . . tinn'd* in the *Elements*.' The
' house of light ' too, simply and inevitably as it
appears here, belongs to astrology.[4] And not only so,

---

[1] Boehme, *The Three Principles*, p. 105.   [2] II, 448.
[3] ' Cock-crowing,' II, 488.
[4] Thomas Vaughan is thought to be the author of a little book called
Aula Lucis, which appeared in 1652, subscribed ' S.N. a Modern Speculator.'
Internal evidence of style points to him, as well as Wood's ascription
(*Athenae Oxonienses*, III, col. 724).

but there is a further close correspondence between this poem and Thomas Vaughan's *Anima Magica Abscondita*, where the author describes a certain ' *Spirituall Metaphysicall Graine*,' a ' Seed or Glance of *Light*,'[1] which guides the ' universall *spirit* of Nature '[2] ' in her Operations' ;[3] and this ' Seed,' or ' Glance,' is descended from the ' *first Father of Lights*.'[4]

> Father of lights ! what Sunnie seed,
> What glance of day hast thou confin'd
> Into this bird !

—so Henry Vaughan's poem begins. His brother continues : ' For though his *full-ey'd* Love shines on nothing but Man, yet every thing in the World is in some measure directed for his Preservation by a *Spice* or *touch* of the *first Intellect*.'[5] And then we find that this further image from the prose treatise has its parallel too in the poem ; but that there, after a fashion we shall have again to notice, the poet has for his own case reversed the relations described, of man as chief recipient of divine light and love, and the rest of Nature recipient only to assist man's ' Preservation ' ; and that while, impelled by that ' immortal light and heat ' ' Whose hand so shines through all this frame ' of the world, the bird's ' Pulse ' ' beats still for light,' he, Vaughan himself, is hampered by a ' veil.'

> This veyle thy full-ey'd love denies,
> And onely gleams and fractions spies.[6]

Vaughan always transmutes his Hermetic tradition in some personal and intimate manner. His cock here

---

[1] T. Vaughan, *Anima Magica Abscondita*, p. 13.
[2] Ibid., p. 10.   [3] Ibid., p. 13.
[4] *Anima Magica Abscondita*, p. 13.   [5] Ibid.
[6] Again, in another of Thomas Vaughan's treatises, there is mention of ' a Veil over the Face,' with which ' We are all born.' And ' This is it, which hinders the prospect of that Intellectual shining Light, which God hath placed in us ' (*Anthroposophia Theomagia*, pp. 37–38).

' dreams of Paradise ' because all the creatures in his
world—sun, stars, birds, and all of Nature except
man—are pictured as belonging in some sort to that
Eden-life of which we have spoken, and which symbolises Vaughan's own desire. But meanwhile the
cock also ' dreams of light ' because, according to
Hermetic tradition, he is a ' solary ' bird, and under the
special influence of the sun.

> To all the breed
> This busie Ray thou hast assign'd ;
> Their magnetisme works all night,
> And dreams of Paradise and light.

And here we are brought to those Hermetic theories
of ' sympathy,' ' magnetism,' and ' influence,' which
underlie so many of his poems, and are themselves
underpropped in his case by a fundamental personal
emotion.

In the threefold world of the Hermetists, the terrestrial, celestial, and intellectual spheres are linked in one,
as in the philosophy of Plotinus each lower grade of
being involves a higher grade on which it is dependent.
And thus each creature in the terrestrial sphere is a
type of some higher creature ; for ' Everywhere there
is an unbroken system of correspondence.   Every
object in the material world is an analogue, a symbol or
counterpart, of some higher reality in the starry heavens,
and this again of some law of the angelic life in the
world beyond the stars.'[1] Each creature bears the
' character ' or hieroglyph of its star ; it bears a
' signature,' which determines its outward form. The
' signature,' another term in the occult philosophy, is,
as Boehme describes it, ' the Receptacle, Container
or Cabinet of the Spirit ' ;[2] and ' The whole outward

---

[1] W. Pater, *The Renaissance*, p. 49 (Chapter on Pico della Mirandola).
[2] Boehme, *Signatura Rerum*, p. 2.

visible World with all its Being is a Signature, or
Figure of the inward spiritual World ' ;[1] or, in Thomas
Vaughan's account, ' The inferior principles bear
witness of the superior. They are signatures and created
books where wee may reade the mysteries of the
supernaturall Trinitie.'[2] The stars and planets take
the sublunary world in charge, and each planet has
as it were a ' cure ' of small terrestrial ' souls.' ' Every
thing therefore hath its Character pressed upon it by
its Star for some peculiar effect, especially by that
Star which doth principally govern it : And these
Characters contain, and retain in them the peculiar
natures, vertues, and roots of their Stars, and produce
the like operations upon other things, on which they
are reflected.'[3] So the cock in Vaughan's poem has
the power, being a solary bird, of reacting to the sun's
first ray, and its own ' magnetism ' draws that ray ;
while other planets and stars shed influence on other
magnetic creatures. ' There is not an *Herb* here *below*,
but he hath a *star* in *Heaven above*, and the *star* strikes
him with her *Beame* and sayes to him, *Grow*.'[4] Thomas
Vaughan visualises the event (which modern science
says may have taken a thousand years to happen)[5]
with the quick child-like imagination of a poet. His
poet-brother writes how some ' kinde herbs '—' kind '
in that word's original sense—' Watch for, and know
their loving star.'[6] Both of them meditate this inter-
action—the ' magnetism ' of the plant attracting the

---

[1] Ibid., p. 77.   [2] Agrippa, pp. 65–66.
[3] T. Vaughan, *Magia Adamica*,   [4] T. Vaughan, *Lumen de Lumine*,
   p. 96.   p. 88.
   [5] ' The light from a distant star is absorbed by a molecule of chlorophyl
which has recently been produced in a living plant. We say that the light
from the star was on its way towards us a thousand years ago. What rapport
can there be between the emitting source and the newly-made molecule of
chlorophyl ? ' (G. N. Lewis, *The Anatomy of Science* (Oxford, 1926), pp.
129–30.)
   [6] ' The Favour,' II, 492.

D

star ; the ' influence ' of the star directing the plant ; the mutual ' sympathy ' which exists between them— with peculiarly loving interest.

> Look up then to *Heaven*, and when thou seest the *Celestiall fires* move in their swift and glorious *Circles*, think also there are here *below* some *cold Natures*, which they *over look*, and about which they *move* incessantly to *heat*, and *concoct* them.[1]

The ' natures ' are of course only *elementally* cold, like the object of the star in Henry Vaughan's poem addressed to that star.

> there's in it a restless, pure desire
> And longing for thy bright and vitall fire,
>   Desire that never will be quench'd,
>   Nor can be writh'd, nor wrench'd.[2]

Vaughan does more than entertain these beliefs in thought. He lives them in emotion, and then images them in poetry. The result lies not so much in frequency of direct reference to Hermetic tradition as in a charging of his poetic atmosphere with this idea of ' sympathy.' Meeting, as we think, some predisposition in himself, it becomes an intuitive knowledge, like an inward sense of touch, directed towards the objects of Nature.

[1] T. Vaughan, *Magia Adamica*, Sig. B5b.
[2] ' The Starre,' II, 489.

V

When I take up a stone or clod of earth and look upon it ;
then I see that which is above, and that which is below, yea,
the whole world therein.[1]

THIS is Jacob Boehme's extended theory of the
microcosm ; Vaughan would have endorsed it ; Traherne too writes of the wonders to be found in a
' grain of sand.'[2] ' You never enjoy the world aright,
till you see how a sand exhibiteth the wisdom and power
of God.' Emile Boutroux in an essay on Boehme
discusses the latter's outlook upon Nature :

> The stars, the sun, the elements of the earth, life every-
> where, in its origin and in every one of its phases, the growing
> tree, the animal with its desires and disinterested instincts,
> man with his inner life . . . all these things Boehme contem-
> plates and meditates upon, and in this immediate and religious
> communion with nature, waits for her to infuse into him her
> own spirit and reveal the mysteries of being. It is eternal,
> interior, and living being that he seeks everywhere and in all
> things. Thus, the phenomena of Nature . . . are signs for
> him to decipher, not the object about which knowledge is
> sought.[3]

Vaughan too is seeking interior and eternal being in

---

[1] Boehme, *Mysterium Magnum*, p. 4.   [2] Traherne, *Centuries*, p. 19.
[3] Boutroux, *Historical Studies in Philosophy*, trans. Rothwell, p. 174. So
Boehme's seventeenth-century biographer relates how ' going abroad into the
Fields . . . and viewing the Herbs and Grass of the field, in his inward Light,
he saw into their Essences, use and properties. . . . In like manner did he
behold the whole Creation ' (*The Life of Jacob Behmen*, by Durand Hotham,
Sig. D3a).

Nature, and, as we have found, he does not image Nature for the sake of the phenomenal object as such alone. In this sense for him as for Boehme natural phenomena are ' signs . . . to decipher,' and books carrying upon them the mysterious signature.

> Thrice happy he who, not mistook,
> Hath read in *Natures mystic Book*.[1]

So Marvell wrote in the lines ' Upon Appleton House.' And the idea of the ' Book of Nature ' or the ' Book of the Creatures ' is an old one, though the Book itself shows variant readings. We may trace some of these backward a little way.

If we should first ask in what form ' Nature ' appears in the literature of Vaughan's or the preceding age, we should find a variety of images clustering round, roughly speaking, two or three conceptions. There is nothing so great and single at once as the figure in Plotinus of the giant creatress, herself under higher compulsion, and brooding ' inactive ' on a vision which is self-intuition,[2] though the massive, elusive being of Spenser's *Mutabilitie* cantos is the nearest to her in stature. On the other hand there is nothing quite like the Nature of the Romantic writers, for seventeenth century ' Nature ' is still partly under the dominion of theology and scholasticism. ' Nature ' might be, vaguely and platonically, the ' body of God ' ; or God and Nature might be identified even, as in Spinoza ; or Nature might be ' the *Instrument* of the still Eternity, wherewith it formeth, maketh and distinguisheth, and therein compacteth itself into a kingdom of joy.'[3] Donne, with his concrete imagination and his love of hierarchies in Church and State, presents a lesser figure—Nature as God's ' Vice-

---

[1] Marvell, p. 77.
[2] Plotinus, trans. Mackenna, II, 123.
[3] Boehme, *Concerning the Election*, p. 12.

gerent,'[1] or his ' owne Lieutenant.'[2] Agrippa describes
a ' magicianess ' who understands the hid dispositions
of matter, and knows how to bring all into a harmony.[3]
Thomas Vaughan, who writes much of Nature,
pictures her now as a goddess, receiving him as devotee
into her temple,[4] now as a wayward and bewitching
being, sporting with herself as ' *Little Children*, who
are newly come from under *her hand* ' can sport—' a
free spirit, that seeks no Applause . . . pleased with
her *own Magic*, as *Philosophers* are with their *Secret*
Philosophie,' and ' busie, not onely in the *Potts* of
the *Balconies*, but in *Wildernesses*, and ruinous *places*
where no *eyes* observe her, but the *Starrs* and *Planets*.'[5]
Vaughan the poet does not present a philosophical
conception; he writes himself that he ' attends upon '
Nature rather than ' speculates.'[6] He does not even
personify this ' Nature ' in a complete image. But he
never sees her other than personally, and alive and
sentient through all her parts the creatures.

> my volumes sed
> They were all dull, and dead,
> They judg'd them senselesse, and their state
> Wholly inanimate.
> Go, go ; Seal up thy looks,
> And burn thy Books.[7]

' Seal up thy looks,' because he is searching for the
invisible world, not ' The skinne, and shell of things ' ;[8]
but on the other hand, ' burn thy Books,' because the

[1] Donne, *XXVI Sermons*, p. 52.
[2] Ibid., ' Goodfriday, 1613, Riding Westward,' *Poems*, I, 336.
[3] Agrippa, p. 74.
[4] T. Vaughan, in *Lumen de Lumine*.
[5] T. Vaughan, *Magia Adamica*, pp. 91–92.
[6] See letter to Aubrey, Vaughan, II, 672.
[7] ' And do they so ? Have they a Sense ? ' II, 432.
[8] ' The Search,' II, 407.

creatures can only be known through loving, immediate intercourse.

There is an old *Liber Creatorum* written by that Raymond of Sebonde[1] whom Montaigne translated, and who but for Montaigne might be now quite forgotten. In that ' Book ' of his, each creature appears as a letter made by the finger of God, and man the chief letter ;[2] but, though the writer stresses the accepted superiority of man to the rest of the creatures man will do well to learn from that Book, for in so far as he studies it, he may the better know himself and God. Withdrawing himself from the creatures, he loses touch with both himself and God.[3] Donne knew Sebonde,[4] and possibly others in Donne's age might know him ; there are passages not unlike things in the *Centuries of Meditations*, though unsuffused with Traherne's peculiar radiance of temper. Yet the Spanish writer's love of Nature is apparent, and suggests some intimacy, and makes that part of his book which deals with the ' creatures ' superior in interest to the strictly theological part. He does not suggest—for though not narrowly scholastic he is orthodox here—anything animistic in the universe. The flower does not *enjoy* the air it breathes. Even with Traherne the rejoicing of Nature has no independence of the soul of man ; and Henry More, whose tenderness grieves over ' fading plants,'[5] knows still that these have no conscious life. ' They never found Themselves when first they peer'd in sunny day ; Nor never sought them-

---

[1] ' A Spaniard, who about two hundred years since professed Physicke in Thoulouse.' (Montaigne, trans. Florio, II, 129.)

[2] Sebonde. Prologue, Sig. A2a.

[3] ' quia quanto magis appropinquas te ad creaturas eas cognoscendo tanto magis appropinquabis ad te ipsum et ad tuum conditorem. Et quanto magis elongas te a creaturis tanto magis elongas te a teipso et a tuo conditore.' (Sebonde, Tit. LIX, Sig. E1b.)

[4] *Essayes in Divinity*, pp. 7–8.   [5] More, *Psychathanasia*, p. 26.

selves ' ;[1] and though trees have ' life Sympatheticall,'
they have no ' animadversive sense '[2] to feel and react.
Yet the lingering ' soul ' of Vaughan's tree in ' The
Timber ' feels dimly the presence of ' great storms '
in Nature, with a ' strange resentment ' like that with
which in the occult tradition the ' astral soul ' of the
dead might resent an injury to its corpse, or as that
corpse itself might ' animadvert ' to the presence
of its murderer.

Man, pleads the old Spanish writer, should love
the creatures as their brother. ' Illas enim debet amare,
et cogitare similitudines quam habet et fraternitatem.'[3]
He pictures them as endeavouring to persuade man
that in taking their services he should recognise them,
and that it is his part to intercede and give thanks not
only for himself but for all the creatures.[4] Such appears
the natural point of view for the religiously-minded in
Vaughan's own century ; for ' one singular End of
man's creation is that he may be a *Priest* in this mag-
nificent *Temple* of the *Universe,* and send up Prayers
and praises to the great Creator of all things in behalf
of the rest of the Creatures.'[5] And is not man ' the
Centre of the Creatures, and the Circle of them all ' ?
' For all things in the world doe not onely look to him
as their Guide and Governour, for whom also they
were all created ; but like wise on him all the Sphaeres
bestow their beams, operations, reflections and in-
fluences, and on him all the Creatures poure their
vertues and effects as upon a middle Point and Retin-
acle or that by which they are stayed and supported.'[6]

[1] More, *Psychathanasia,* p. 11.   [2] Ibid., p. 14.
[3] Sebonde, Tit. LIX, Sig. E1a.
[4] Ibid., Tit. XCVI, Sig. G3b. With his ' Et sic omnes creature clamant
et testificantur,' etc., compare Traherne's ' They daily cry in a living manner,
with a silent and yet most loud voice, We are all His gifts.' (*Centuries*, p. 101.)
[5] More, *An Antidote against Atheism,* p. 85.
[6] Oswald Crollius, *The Mysteries of Nature*, p. 56.

The picture given by the ' chemist ' Crollius suggests vividly an astrological diagram.

It is rather noteworthy that Sebonde's translator, with his infinite curiosity and his indifference to accepted standards, reverses these positions. Through ' vanity ' alone man, ignoble and dependent as he is, ' ascribeth divine conditions unto himselfe,' and ' selecteth and separateth himselfe from out the ranks of other creatures ; to which his fellow-brethren and compeers, he cuts out and shareth their parts . . . How knoweth he by the vertue of his understanding the inward and secret motions of beasts ? '[1] But to most, even the sensitive, of the seventeenth century, the creatures, whether for beauty or for use, have little or no significance apart from man. Donne could hardly be expected to be anything but incredulous of the legend of St. Francis. ' They will needs make us believe, that St. *Francis* preached to Birds, and Beasts, and Stones ; but they will not go about to make us believe that those Birds, and Beasts, and Stones joyned with *St. Francis* in prayer . . . of all onely Man can speak to God.'[2] George Herbert, who himself loved and marked the life of Nature, writes in ' Providence ' :

> Beasts fain would sing ; birds dittie to their notes ;
> Trees would be tuning on their native lute
> To thy renown ; but all their hands and throats
> Are brought to Man, while they are lame and mute.[3]

Then, repeating the thought we have already met in More and Sebonde, he proceeds :

> Man is the world's high Priest. He doth present
> The sacrifice for all.

And Vaughan echoes Herbert, as he so often echoes

[1] Montaigne, trans. Florio, II, 144.   [3] Herbert, III, 79.
[2] Donne, *XXVI Sermons*, p. 31.

him, in his poem called ' Christ's Nativity '[1]—' Man
is their high-priest.' But immediately afterwards he
forgoes his office, and begins to plead himself the least
of their disciples.

> I would I were some *Bird* or Star,
> Flutt'ring in woods, or lifted far
> Above this *Inne*
> And Rode of sin !
> Then either Star, or *Bird*, should be
> Shining, or singing still to thee.

Or again,

> I would I were a stone, or tree,
> Or flowre by pedigree,
> Or some poor high-way herb, or Spring
> To flow, or bird to sing. . . .[2]

The ' ladder ' with which good Catholics begin their
Books of Nature is reversed in his poetry, and ' All
have their *keyes,* and set *ascents* ' ; but man ' Sleeps at
the ladders foot.'[3] For the creatures all move in harmony ; they have kept their magic correspondence.

> Thy other Creatures in this Scene
> Thee only aym, and mean ;[4]

> But I am sadly loose, and stray
> A giddy blast each way ;[5]

There are ' some stones ' which even ' in the darkest
nights point to their homes ' ;[6] but man, in theology
and cosmology the centre of the universe, has lost his
way, and ' knocks at all doors, strays and roams.'[7]

---

[1] II, 442.
[2] ' And do they so ? Have they a Sense ?' II, 432.
[3] ' The Tempest,' II, 461.
[4] ' And do they so ? Have they a Sense ?' II, 432.
[5] Ibid.
[6] ' Man,' II, 477. [7] Ibid.

And ' hearts are not so kind,' i.e., ' true to their heavenly kin,' as herbs.[1]

Here in passing we may notice that Bunyan amidst his spiritual conflicts finds man, though ' the most noble by Creation of all creatures in the visible World,' changed by sin to ' the most ignoble.' ' The beasts, birds, fishes, etc., I blessed their condition, for they had not a sinful nature, they were not obnoxious to the wrath of God.'[2] And in Rámon Lull's *Tree of Love*, the Lover and the ' ladies of love ' turn away from the city ; ' And their will was to leave the world, and to be no more among men, but rather to dwell with birds, beasts and trees, for these dishonour not the Beloved.'[3] Vaughan is not without antecedents and parallels in his notice and love of Nature, but the love itself appears differently compounded. It appears unique in its consistent attitude of discipleship, and in that ' sympathy ' we have tried to describe which, trained in the Hermetic tradition as it is, we recognise for inherent and instinctive. When—in the familiar picture of ' The Retreate '—

> on some gilded *Cloud,* or *flowre*
> My gazing soul would dwell an houre,
> And in those weaker glories spy
> Some shadows of eternity[4]

he is apprehending in the way that Traherne apprehends in the *Centuries*. But whereas Traherne or Henry More seem to drink in beauty above all from the eye—

> Fresh varnish'd groves, tall hills, and gilded clouds
> Arching an eielid for the gloring morn[5]

—and so make the rarified sense of sight chief mediator to their central joy, Vaughan himself might be said,

---

[1] ' Sure, there's a tye of Bodyes ! ' II, 429.
[2] Bunyan, *Grace Abounding*, p. 321.
[3] Rámon Lull, *The Tree of Love*, trans. Peers, p. 99.
[4] II, 419.   [5] More, *Psychathanasia*, p. 62.

like More's own 'Psyche,' to see by 'tactuall' sight,[1] not needing so much the 'secondary '[2] kind of vision. His world indeed is made up of outward vision and of the dream directing it, through which he feels his way to the heart of the creatures, to the dim spark of sentience which he thinks still lurks in the dead timber ;[3] the vital spark which kindles the cock, the bird of dawning ;[4] or the wisdom of the smaller nesting bird pillowing its head on its wing through a night of storm.[5] Turning back to the obscure Spaniard's *Book of the Creatures*, we find Sebonde saying that man to explore these creatures fully should '*fricare animam suam cum eis.*'[6] Vaughan does—in this quaint phrase—'rub his soul against'[7] the creatures; and strives with the common desire of the mystic to pass within his object, as at the end of his poem 'The Night' he strives to pass within the Divine. There is a poem in the second part of *Silex Scintillans* called.'The Book,'[8] which reveals this intimacy with a curious beauty, quiet, matter-of-fact, but almost startling. The 'Book' is here an actual volume, on which the poet's 'gazing soul' has fallen, while he meditates backward through its history to the once living material of which it is made, which lived in the Divine regard, and, he would think, in some sense lives so still.

> Thou knew'st this *papyr*, when it was
> Meer *seed*, and after that but *grass* ;
> Before 'twas *drest*, or *spun*, and when
> Made *linen*, who did *wear* it then :

---

[1] Ibid., p. 61.
[2] Ibid., p. 61.
[3] 'The Timber,' II, 497.
[4] 'Cock-crowing,' II, 488.
[5] 'The Bird,' II, 496.
[6] Sebonde, Tit. LIX, Sig. E1a.
[7] My attention was drawn to this phrase and to a study of Sebonde himself through reading Prof. C. C. J. Webb's *Studies in the History of Natural Theology* (Oxford, 1915).
[8] II, 540.

. . . Thou knew'st this *Tree*, when a green *shade*
Cover'd it, since a *Cover* made,
And where it flourish'd, grew and spread,
As if it never should be dead.

Thou knew'st this harmless *beast*, when he
Did live and feed by thy decree
On each green thing ; then slept (well fed)
Cloth'd with this *skin*, which now lies spred
A *Covering* o're this aged book.

. . . Thou knew'st and saw'st them all and though
Now scatter'd thus, dost know them so. . . .

VI

To penetrate such poems as ' The Book,' ' The Timber,' or ' The Bird ' is to perceive the difference between Vaughan and his predecessors, and the peculiar quality of his thought and art. We read other poems, or read his prose translations, and for all the fineness and dignity of his prose and the unwarranted additions too that come at intervals to remind the reader that his own thought kept pace with his translation and informed it,[1] and for all his loyalty and indignation as an Anglican and the numerous poems expressing a devotion which is wistful of the peace the Anglican Church might give, we may still be best satisfied to know him as one of mixed and only half-conscious allegiances ; as one who perhaps in another age might have expressed his love of Nature without tradition Catholic or Hermetic.[2] Yet as far as our acquaintance can go, we see him gaining by his traditions. They make him on many sides a more sensitive beholder.

As for his specifically religious experiences, the likeness to Herbert fades on a nearer and more detailed view. Beyond that desire we have described which became conscious in his conversion, and which from vague searchings or quiet expectation deepens in ' The Night ' to an embodiment in image of the culmination of desire, Vaughan is less sharply aware of

---

[1] For these additions, see the notes to Martin's edition.
[2] W. H. Hudson finds in Traherne ' a poetry which was distinctly animistic, with Christianity grafted on it' (*Far Away and Long Ago*, Chapter XVII, p. 235). Would he have proposed the same for Henry Vaughan ?

his spiritual states than Herbert, or Donne, or Bunyan. He does not suffer the terror of alienation as they do, nor in quite such an intimate and personal manner the joy of redemption under the symbol of the Cross. His religious experiences do not appear as acutely-defined problems or conflicts. There is indeed the note of exile, but there is nothing like the agony described in Herbert's ' Denial '—

> O, that thou shoudst give dust a tongue
>   To crie to thee,
> And then not heare it crying ! All day long
>   My heart was in my knee,
>   But no hearing.[1]

or the tremendous appeal of Donne's ' Batter my heart, three-person'd God,'[2] which expresses the desire of all intense and self-conscious souls to feel the hand of mastery. It is true that in the Emblem to his book Vaughan uses an image which resembles that of the ' usurp'd town to another due ' of Donne's sonnet.

> Thy siege comes sharper ; by Thy shock
>   My wall's o'er thrown ;
> Thou shatter'st even my breast of rock,
>   And what was stone
>   Is flesh and blood. . . .[3]

[1] Herbert, II, 299.
[2] *Holy Sonnets*, XIV, Donne, Poems, I, 328.
[3] Blunden's translation. *On the Poems of Henry Vaughan*, p. 62. Those interested in the relations between Henry and Thomas Vaughan might compare the Emblem to *Silex Scintillans* with a poem in the latter's *Anthroposophia Theomagia*, p. 28. There too is imaged the ' stone ' become a ' springing well,' and the flint waiting for the fire of God.

> Lord God ! This was a *stone*,
> as *hard* as any *One*
> Thy *Laws* in *Nature* fram'd :
> 'Tis now a *springing Well*,
> and many Drops can tell,
> Since it by *Art* was tam'd.

But the sense of a divine impact comes, we think, differently to him than to Donne. Donne in his religion loves contrast, light and shade ; and to feel the great gulf between creature and creator. His sense of sin is heightened by his need of contrast ; and his God is imaged as both intensely personal and also intensely numinous. His vision is what has been called ' prophetic '1 or ' Hebraic,' while Vaughan's is mystical, and the outcome of a need for union with the object of his worship. His God is seldom so personal and never so austere as Donne's. The image at the end of ' The Night ' is rather that of the great Uncreated and Uncreating of some older mystics.

And to Vaughan man appears as an exile from Paradise ; to others of Vaughan's century man is not only exile, he is refugee ; his depravity is stressed by Catholics such as Donne and Pascal, and Puritans such as Baxter and Bunyan ; and the Fall is an outstanding fact, whether viewed literally and historically, or as with Boehme, some Hermetists and ' Platonic ' writers, and perhaps some Quakers, mainly psycho-

---

My God ! my *Heart* is so,
'tis all of Flint, and no
Extract of *Teares* will yeeld :
Dissolve it with thy *Fire*,
that something may *aspire*,
And *grow* up in my *Field*.

Bare teares Ile not intreat,
But let thy *Spirits seat*
Upon these *Waters* bee,
That *I new form'd* with *Light*
shall move without all *Night*
Or *Excentricity.*

¹ For an illuminating distinction between these two types of religious response, compare *Pascal's Philosophy of Religion*, by C. C. J. Webb (Oxford, 1929), p. 29 ff.

logically and mystically.[1] In Nieremberg, the Jesuit writer whose *De Árte Voluntatis* Vaughan translated under the title *Of Life and Death*, the soul of man, like that same soul pictured in the *Theologia Germanica*,[2] sees itself as lower than the devils. ' For they did not sin against a God, who for their Sakes became an Angel, neither had they such a ful proof of his goodness : they did not sin against a God, who for them vouchsafed to be crucified : they did not sin against a God who made himself the food of their soules . . . But I have sinn'd . . . against a God . . . who dy'd for me, who wept for me upon the cross with loud out-cryes, and not a joint of his body but bewailed each of my offences in the garden with teares of blood.'[3]

So Donne writes in one of the *Holy Sonnets*—

> For I have sinn'd, and sinn'd, and onely hee,
> Who could do no iniquitie, hath dyed.[4]

The thought of original sin is constant with Donne as with Augustine ; though Vaughan, we remember, is intent on his ' Angell-infancy,'[5] and on the ' Remnant of Paradise,'[6] lingering there. Vaughan's poetry too is, as his brother said, ' conversant '[7] with angels ; nor is that converse alien to an age which loved to

---

[1] E.g., Joseph Glanville, More's disciple, describes a Fall after the manner of Cabbalistic or Gnostic speculation (*Lux Orientalis*, p. 144 ff). ' Adam ' (a representative figure) sleeps ; and there is a remission of the higher powers of the soul. Then ' Eve,' the lower life, is brought forth ; and the body awakes. But Adam is still innocent, and still in Paradise, until the delights of the body betray him, and he falls from Paradise to inhabit the region of the air. A still further descent takes place in souls who are attracted towards the grosser pleasures of the lower earth.

[2] *Theologia Germanica*, trans. Winkworth, p. 33.

[3] Nieremberg, *Of Adoration in Spirit and in Truth*, p. 49 ff.

[4] *Holy Sonnets*, XI. Donne, *Poems*, I, 327.

[5] ' The Retreate,' II, 419.   [6] See p. 28.

[7] T. Vaughan, *Magia Adamica*, p. 2. Thomas Vaughan uses the word to describe the relations between God and ' magicians,' the earliest ' magicians ' being, according to tradition, the patriarchs.

speculate, to classify, to discuss the composition of angels, their hierarchies, and their exalted, extreme felicities. The *Silex* angels, however, do not much frequent the empyrean. They are rustics and spirits of the grove ; ' Each Oke and high-way knew them.'[1] They are shy spirits, whom ' foul men ' can ' drive away ' ;[2] but they are sociable with children, and even play with them.[3] If in his reading Vaughan had ever met Jacob Boehme's description of the angels, he must have loved its unconventional and tender gaiety.

> I will liken them to little *Children*, which walk in the fields in May, among the *flowers*, and pluck them, and make curious *Garlands*, and *Poseys*, carrying them in their hands *rejoycing*.[4]

One of the attractions of the life to come to Boehme is that ' We shall lead a life like children, who rejoyce and are very merry in their Sports,' and shall pass the time in ' a delightfull Recreation with the Angels.'[5] ' There is such a kind of dancing and singing, as Children use when they hold hands, and sing and dance a round.'[6] And in Vaughan's own ' Palm-Sunday,' while the children cry Hosanna,

> their own Angels shine and sing
> In a bright ring :
> Such yong, sweet mirth
> Makes heaven and earth
> Joyn in a joyful Symphony.[7]

To Vaughan, again, the symbol of refuge for man is ' home ' or ' Eden,' as the Church is the sanctuary for that bird—a swallow, the swallow of Psalm LXXXIV— to which George Herbert compares his soul.

---

[1] ' Corruption,' II, 440.
[2] ' Childe-hood,' II, 521.
[3] Ibid.

[4] Boehme, *Aurora*, p. 239.
[5] Boehme, *XL Questions*, p. 129.
[6] Ibid., pp. 129–30.
[7] II, 501.

> O let me, when thy roof my soul hath hid,
> O let me roost and nestle there.[1]

But above all, to Puritan Bunyan, or Donne, or Herbert, or Nieremberg, or that other Jesuit writer whom also Vaughan probably knew, Hieremias Drexelius, the refuge for man the refugee is the love of Christ as redeemer.

> Remember, sweet Jesus, that thou didst spread thy armes abroad upon the crosse, openedst thy breast, & didst hang down thy head. Beholde my soule forsaken by all creatures seekes refuge, and casts itself into those armes, and insinuates itself into that breast of thine.[2]

The Christ of the best poems in *The Temple*, of ' Love,'[3] for instance, or ' The Bag,'[4] is a very tender, human-hearted, and rather whimsical person, imaged with a mingling of familiarity with reverence, of the attitude of the humble with that of the privileged lover. Donne shows the heroic impetuosity of a Christ who could ' Come so in-gloriously . . . come . . . so selfe proditoriously ' to the redemption of man,[5] or the ' picture of Christ crucified,' where the wrath which for Donne always darkens and enhances the Divine is submerged in love, and ' Teares in his eyes quench the amazing light.'[6] Traherne sees Christ on the cross, where ' To this poor, bleeding, naked Man did all the corn and wine, and oil, and gold and silver in the world minister in an invisible manner, even as he was exposed lying and dying upon the Cross.'[7]

The image at the end of Vaughan's ' The Night,' the ' deep but dazling darkness,' expresses, as we have seen, his fundamental desire. It is his special

---

[1] ' The Temper.' Herbert, II, 317.
[2] Drexelius, *The Angel-Guardian's Clock*, p. 114.
[3] Herbert, II, 401.
[4] Ibid., III, 157.

[5] Donne, *LXXX Sermons*, p. 65.
[6] Ibid. *Holy Sonnets*, XIII, Poems, I, 328.
[7] Traherne, *Centuries*, p. 43.

apprehension of ' Christian annihilation . . . in-
gression into the divine shadow ' ;[1] though not neces-
sarily Christian in its inception. But his human Christ
remains still the figure of the first stanzas of ' The
Night,' of ' The Dwelling-place,'[2] and ' Palm-Sunday.'
Among the inhabitants of his world, the dead who
dispense light like stars ;[3] the stars and magnetic
herbs and mysterious, heaven-directed stones ; God-
intoxicated birds ; children, angels, or the ' harmless,
yong and happy Ass,'[4] that carried Christ on Palm
Sunday, is the figure of Christ himself, the dweller
by ' secret fountain ' or ' Fair Shade,'[5] or under the
' unhaunted ' ' Tent ' of night.[6] He too like his poet
is merged into his surroundings and identified with
them. When in ' Palm-Sunday ' appeal is made to the
' Plants of the day,' ' Whom sufferings,' i.e. storms,
' make most green and gay,' it is because

> The King of grief, the man of sorrow,
> Weeping still, like the wet morrow,
> Your shades and freshness comes to borrow.[7]

He is imaged as an opening flower ' Within whose
sacred leafs did lie The fulness of the Deity ' ;[8] his
quality is that freshness and perennial youth which
Vaughan loved in Nature and longed to recapture.

> Early, while yet the *dark* was gay,
> And *gilt* with stars, more trim than day :
> Heav'ns *Lily,* and the Earth's chast *Rose :*
> The green, Immortal BRANCH arose ;
> And in a solitary place
> Bow'd to his father his bless'd face.[9]

[1] Browne, *Hydriotaphia,* p. 83.   [2] II, 516.
[3] Compare ' Joy of my life ! While left me here,' II, 423 ; ' They are all
gone into the world of light,' II, 484.
[4] ' Palm-Sunday,' II, 502.   [5] ' The Dwelling-Place,' II, 516.
[6] ' The Night,' II, 523.   [7] II, 501.
[8] ' The Night,' II, 522.   [9] ' The Day-spring,' II, 643.

Exploring a little further the chief paths of seventeenth-century religious thought, we find that Vaughan's attitude towards the fact of death is relevant for mention here ; because, though Vaughan's age made death its theme, and though, curiously enough, he chose for his own library an author like Nieremberg and perhaps too Drexelius, writers whose melancholy and often piercing tone is insistent on death and damnation, he himself does not in *Silex Scintillans* assume such tones. Death means corruption, but it also means unification. Here when alive man is indeed ' crumbled dust,'[1] or a ' heap of sand,'[2] loose and shifting, in the vagrancy and dulness of his desires, which render him incapable of steady radiance of achievement like that for instance of ' a pearle, a starre, or a rainbow.'[3] The poem called ' Distraction ' is an excellent example of an approved metaphysical feat, rarely so accomplished in this poet ; but through-out the poem Vaughan's need for the unifying experience is clearly shown.

As regards the dust of death, he finds that ' The Dust, of which I am a part ' is one of ' Thy Creatures ' ;[4] and death is a ' Change of suits.'[5]

> For no thing can to *Nothing* fall, but still
> Incorporates by skill,
> And then returns, and from the wombe of things
> Such treasure brings
> As *Phenix*-like renew'th
> Both life, and youth.[6]

The difference between his and the general con-temporary attitude towards death appears due to his intuition of Earth and of this ' preserving spirit '[7]

---

[1] ' Distraction,' II, 413.
[2] ' Church-Service,' II, 426.
[3] ' Distraction.'
[4] ' Repentance,' II, 448–9.

[5] ' Resurrection and Immortality,' II, 401.
[6] Ibid.
[7] Ibid.

which causes Nature and humanity, ' Phenix-like,' to renew their being. In some poems that deal with resurrection the expected event appears natural as morning, or the event of Spring, when ' through the dead Creatures a bed ' the ' renewing breath ' is blown.[1] The Day of Judgment even is

> A day so fresh, so bright, so brave,
> Twill show us each forgotten grave,
> And make the dead, like flowers, arise
> Youthful and fair to see new skies[2]

i.e., the ' new heaven ' and ' new earth ' of the Apocalypse. In fact, the dead in Vaughan's poetry are always young, and have attained to those states of simplicity, beauty and peace towards which the poet himself is always yearning. They are ' shining lights ' ; [3] they shed influence ' Like stars upon some gloomy grove,'[4] or like a song listened to in thought after the bird has flown.[5] The soul of a dead infant of whom he writes is like a bird that ' Flew home unstain'd by his new kin.'[6] Another one, perhaps a dead brother, the brother whose death Thomas Vaughan mentions in *Anthroposophia Theomagia*,[7] is imaged as ' this *Prim-rose* ' ;[8] or in a further poem where the image is more explicit, as a hidden but living and growing flower.

> I digg'd about
> That place where I had seen him to grow out,
> And by and by
> I saw the warm Recluse alone to lie
> Where fresh and green
> He lived of us unseen.

---

[1] ' Resurrection and Immortality,' II, 400.
[2] ' The day of Judgement,' II, 530.
[3] ' Joy of my life ! while left me here,' II, 423.
[4] ' They are all gone into the world of light,' II, 484.
[5] Ibid.
[6] ' The Burial of an Infant,' II, 450.
[7] p. 65.
[8] ' Thou that know'st for whom I mourne,' II, 417.

Many a question Intricate and rare
Did I there strow,
But all I could extort was, that he now
Did there repair
Such losses as befel him in this air
And would e'r long
Come forth most fair and young.[1]

And, as here in the picture of the 'warm recluse,'
✓ Vaughan loves all images that suggest secrecy, greenness, youth, purity, and renewal—the 'Dear secret
Greenness! nurst below Tempests and windes, and
winter nights';[2] the purity of mornings, which in
themselves are 'Mysteries';[3] the mystery of children
'driving' their 'white designs';[4] and the continual
re-births of Nature. His belief in atonement is in an
atonement through return to the source, and so through
re-birth to universal regeneration. It is all a question
— of the return and the re-birth. Among the alchemists
the transmutations of their art were types of re-birth ;
and among Protestants and Quakers the doctrine of
a 'second birth' is important as part of individual
experience. But with Jacob Boehme, and, though
expressed less directly, with Henry Vaughan himself,
re-birth or regeneration appears as the sudden advent,
— or the slower revelation through Nature, of a world-
embracing, atoning Spirit. Beyond the belief lies the
philosophy of St. Paul, and the image of the 'whole
creation' 'travailing' towards a 'glorious liberty.'[5]

And therefore it is that the whole nature standeth in
anguish and longing, to be freed from the vanity. . . . Because
it tasteth the Paradise in it selfe, and in the Paradise the perfection, and therefore it groaneth and lifteth it selfe up towards the light of God and Paradise ; and so bringeth forth

[1] ' I walkt the other day (to spend   [3] ' Rules and Lessons,' II, 436.
my hour),' II, 478.   [4] ' Childe-hood,' II, 520.
[2] ' The Seed growing secretly,' II,   [5] *Romans,* VIII, 19–22.
511.

in its anguish always somewhat that is fairer, higher and
new . . . and if you be not blinde, you may see this in Men,
Beasts, yea even in hearbs and grasse.[1]

The lyric prayer to the ' knowing, glorious spirit ' at
the end of Vaughan's poem ' The Book ' of which we
spoke looks forward to the time when the Spirit shall
' restore trees, beasts and men.'[2] There too the writer
appeals to the ' Rock of Ages,' ' In whose shade They
live unseen, when here they fade '—perhaps a more
Christian rendering, and characteristic of his manner
in mingling traditions, of the belief of Paracelsus in a
' mysterium Magnum,' from which all the creation
was generated, and to which it will all return. In this
' great mystery ' all things, even the smaller creatures,
live after an eternal species.

It is opposed to all true philosophy to say that flowers lack
their own eternity. They may perish and die here ; but they
will re-appear in the restitution of all things. Nothing has been
created out of the great mystery which will not inhabit a
form beyond the aether.[3]

The creatures have, according to this philosopher, a
perishable elemental form, and an eternal form, an
' imago extra aethere,' which shall be given them in a
final ' great Mystery ' (in ultimo mysterio magno),
and by which they will be recognisable. Though
the individual earthly life is to cease, the result is
not unlike the ' glorified body ' of the Christian
resurrection. That ' truly learned and expert Physician,'[4] Oswald Crollius, writes of a regeneration at the
end of the world ' according to Soul, Spirit, and Body,'
when the soul will ' sparkle and glitter out with a
fiery colour like a Rubie or Carbuncle thorow the clear,

[1] Boehme, The Three Principles,
  p. 61.
[2] ' The Book,' II, 540.
[3] Paracelsus, II, 269.
[4] Vaughan (Hermetical Physick),
  II, 584.

spotlesse, beautifull body.'[1] And in the ' Envoy ' to
the second part of *Silex Scintillans* Vaughan presents,
in language reminiscent of biblical image, but in some
sort prophetic of Shelley in *Adonais*,[2] the coming of a
universal radiant redemption.

> Arise, arise !
> And like old cloaths fold up these skies,
> This long worn veyl : then shine and spread
> Thy own bright self over each head,
> And through thy creatures pierce and passe
> Till all becomes thy cloudlesse glass,
> Transparent as the purest day. . . .[3]

[1] Crollius, *The Mysteries of Nature*, p. 138.

[2] *Adonais*, 381–7 ; 462–3.
[3] ' L'Envoy,' II, 542.